COACH GIRLS

MIA WENJEN AND ALISON FOLEY

How to Coach Girls

Text Copyright 2018

Editors: Lydia Davis and Mallory Leonard

Text design: meadencreative.com

Cover design: meadencreative.com

Cover Photography: Zoe Lee

First Edition: 2018

Library of Congress Control Number on File

P-ISBN: 978-1-936426-03-4

Audrey Press
P.O. Box 6113
Maryville, TN 37802

Visit us at www.audreypress.com

Printed in the USA

How to
COACH GIRLS

MIA WENJEN AND ALISON FOLEY

DEDICATIONS

Alison Foley

My ultimate measure of being a good coach is watching girls smile, feel empowered and willing to take risks while feeling supported. My hopes as a mom is that the coaches that come in to my daughter Sidnie's life can realize the gift of coaching girls and the positive impact they can have in her life and many other young women. I want to thank Sidnie for sharing me with so many other girls I coach. You make me a better coach because my love for you reminds me every day the importance I have in coaching and influencing someone else's daughter.

Mia Wenjen

What I've learned from watching my girls play sports and my husband volunteer coach is that coaching is a lot like parenting … a deep dedication to caring about the kids on the team, and a skill to be acquired largely through trial and error. My girls have had the good fortune to be shaped by many wonderful coaches throughout their formative years, and this book is dedicated to all those who give back to their community in the form of coaching. You are all role models, mentors, and cheerleaders to help kids reach their full potential.

CONTENTS

INTRODUCTION

About 70% of kids give up organized sports by the time they reach middle school.*

Girls drop out of sports at six times the rate of boys.**

Only 7% of high school athletes move on to college sports.***

I don't know about you, but we find these statistics to be alarming and disheartening. We know that the benefits of playing sports are numerous for girls. It promotes a positive body image and instills teamwork, leadership, resiliency, humility, and perseverance—all skills that help girls become successful adults. Sport encourages social awareness through community service, self-advocacy, and the ability to be a good follower.

And yet out of 100 girls who play a sport in elementary school, only two will play in college.

So, we wondered, what can be done to retain more girls in sport?

In tackling the issue, we've found that there is an easy solution, one that is backed up by current research*. It comes down to one simple idea: make sports fun *for girls.*

Fun isn't about winning, although winning is fun, so are team rituals and group effort and inspirational coaching.

As we go on to discuss throughout the book, girls have distinct needs within the arena of sport. It's important to girls that they develop a trust relationship with their coach, in which they are viewed as a whole person, as opposed to just an athlete. Creating great team chemistry is also crucial to girls' participation, and it can be done with just a little pre-planning. With this in mind, coaches have the ability to ensure girls return to the sport the following season, and the one after that.

We hope that this book provides coaches, both professional and volunteer parent coaches – the unsung heroes – with an invaluable resource to turn to when preparing for a new season. As a coach, you have a significant ability to impact a girl's life. We applaud you and thank you for caring about developing girls into good people, as well as good athletes.

We are on social media (Twitter, Facebook and Instagram @ HowToCoachGirls) and we have a website HowToCoachGirls. com. We hope that you will contribute your advice or come to us with questions related to coaching girls. We'd love to post your ideas on how you keep your team coming back to play again next season. Thank you for sharing.

Best,

Alison and Mia

*Poll from National Alliance for Youth Sports. Miner, Juliana M. "Why 70% of kids quit sports by age 13?" WashingtonPost.com website. 1 Jun. 2016. Web. The Washington Post. 3 Oct. 2017.

**deLench, Brooke. Home Team Advantage: The Critical Role of Mothers in Youth Sports. New York: Harpers Perennial, 2006.

***Amanda J. Visek, Sara M. Achrati, Heather Manning, Karen McDonnell, Brandonn S. Harris, and Loretta DiPietro. The Fun Integration Theory: Towards Sustaining Children and Adolescents Sport Participation. Journal of Physical Activity and Health. 2015 Mar; 12(3): 424–433.

P.S. OUR BACKSTORY

It all began over ten years ago when Alison moved into a new neighborhood. Her daughter, Sidnie, wanted to be friends with the girls she saw playing outside around the corner from their new house, Zoe and Ali. The three girls became like sisters, including the fighting. Brought together by their daughters, Alison and Mia became friends too.

In the beginning, Zoe, Ali, and Sidnie played soccer, starting with Kindergarten Soccer, which is designed to encourage incoming Kindergarteners to make new friends before school starts. They progressed to town soccer, travel soccer, and club soccer. There was plenty of drama, and Mia consulted Alison—a professional women's soccer coach—at every twist and turn.

As the years went on, these three girls played a multitude of other sports: basketball, softball, rowing, volleyball, surfing, diving, rock climbing, sailing, tennis, skiing, snowboarding, cross country skiing, gymnastics, kickboxing, karate, swimming, rhythm gymnastics, cross country, boxing, lacrosse, track and field, and golf. Different sports, but still a lot of the same drama.

Like an exceptional teacher, your children sometimes are fortunate to get at school, my daughters would also have an outstanding coaching experience that made them fall in love with that sport. As a parenting and education blogger, I share my experiences and resources in hopes it will help others. I knew that my friend, Alison Foley, was exceptionally qualified to share how to successfully coach girls and young women. Not only does she have a degree in sports psychology of girls, but as Boston College's Head Coach of Women's Soccer, I've watched her over the years nurture and develop her players. I asked her to write this book with me and she agreed. In the same way that I was able to get advice from her when I really needed it, I tried to capture her advice on a myriad of issues that I encountered. In addition, we asked fifteen coaches who we think are exceptional at coaching girls and young women to contribute their advice to coaches.

We hope that this book helps parents who coach, parents of girls who play sports, and professional coaches with the ultimate goal: get each girl on the team to want to return the next season.

Alison Foley is the Head Women's Soccer Coach at Boston College. Her team's success has led them to the NCAA Final Four and Final Eight in 13 consecutive play-off appearances. In her 20-year career, she has coached many national team level players.

Alison started playing soccer at a young age. She worked herself through the school and club soccer ranks, receiving ODP regional and national invitations, and was a college All-American. She is now entering her 14th season of Lady Eagles Soccer School. And she still enjoys playing the game.

Alison and Mia also created Alison's brainchild, *Soccer on the Mat* (**socceronthemat.com**), a unique and innovative soccer and yoga program specifically designed for middle school girls.

Mia Wenjen co-founded Aquent in 1986 with two friends as a dorm-room entrepreneur at Harvard University. She has been a member of the Board of Directors ever since and has held a number of roles at the company, including founding the West Coast operations and growing the Los Angeles, California office into the company's largest market. In 1992, Aquent (then called MacTemps) placed #12 on the Inc. 500 list for Fastest Growing Private Company.

Mia is also a blogger at PragmaticMom.com, a mash-up covering education, parenting, and multicultural children's books. Her blog receives over one million views a year. She is a co-founder of Multicultural Children's Book Day, January 27th, a non-profit which celebrates diversity in children's literature. In just three days, the event generated over 3.6 billion social media share impressions!

THE BIG PICTURE

THE BIG PICTURE

1 | The Differences between Coaching Girls and Boys

Mia: *As a mom of two girls and a boy, I would say that coaching boys versus coaching girls is a continuum, and that there are no hard and fast rules of how boys and girls differ. However, I have observed that the coaches of my girls who had the greatest impact were those who took a 'whole child' approach, where the social-emotional connection was emphasized. Alison's slant to this chapter is based both on her own experiences and those of her many friends who coach; together they discussed what they believe are the key differences between coaching girls and boys.*

Alison: The University of North Carolina coach, Anson Dorrance, gave me an invaluable piece of advice when I first started coaching. He advised me to give the girls on the team the first ten minutes of practice. Let them catch-up with each other during this time, and as a result, you will have their full attention for the next eighty minutes of practice. If you don't, they will try to get their ten minutes throughout the entire practice, meaning they are constantly distracted.

I followed his advice and I give my team ten minutes of warm-ups where they can ask each other about tests, boyfriends, room-mate situations, and all the other things that are on their mind. This bonding time is really important for them, and once they have reconnected with each other, they are ready to get to work.

The same theory applies to younger girls who have been sitting in school all day. They want to chat. They need this time at the start of practice to decompress and connect with their teammates.

This is a significant difference in the ways that girls and boys can differ in sports, but it's not the only one. When polling other coaches, the following comparisons emerged from our discussions:

- Girls tend to be better listeners
- Girls are more likely to play for each other
- Girls are more likely to feel an attachment for their coach
- Boys can still perform for a coach to whom they don't feel connected, in a way that girls are unable to
- Boys tend to be braver and more confident
- Girls want to be accepted
- A female player can't be in the unknown, she can't be uncertain about how the coach feels about her
- Girls want you to know them as a whole person, and not just for their abilities as a player
- Girls are more likely to be perfectionists
- Girls tend to doubt their abilities
- Girls are more afraid to fail
- Boys tend to inflate their abilities

Fundamentally, boys tend to be over-confident in their abilities when compared to girls, and this has significant consequences when developing players. Boys tend to think they are better than they actually are, and as a result, they are unafraid to take risks such as partnering with the best player on the team. The confidence to take risks is actually a big factor in developing a player's skills and so I find that I have to take a different approach with girls than I would with boys. I need to create a safe and nurturing environment so that they feel comfortable with the possibility of failing, whether it's in front of me or their teammates. If I have succeeded in developing a nurturing relationship with a player, she's then willing to take risks for me on the field, whether that means playing in a different position, or working on a specific skill that requires her to 'fail' for a long period of time before she masters it.

Girls need you to see them as a 'whole person', not just a player

It's important that I connect with each player on an emotional level, so that she feels that we have a relationship and that I understand her as a complete person, not just a player on the field. Therefore, I'll spend time learning about each athlete's family, her extra-curricular activities, her recent vacation, and, if she trusts me enough, even her relationship issues.

In learning these things about my players, I'm building an emotional connection with each one of them. Seeing them as more than just an athlete is crucial both for the girls and their parents, because parents also want to know that the coach genuinely cares about their daughter and understands that there are other things going on in their lives. And today, there is a lot pressure in all areas of their lives, whether it's grades or relationships or their future.

Fundamentally, my contribution to this book – and this falls solidly within my remit as a Head Coach – is to understand and discuss the social emotional aspect of the Whole Child Approach, an approach which is also embedded in the education system in our public schools:

> *The Whole Child Approach: each child, in each school, in each of our communities deserves to be healthy, safe, engaged, supported, and challenged. That's what a whole child approach to learning, teaching, and community engagement really is.*
>
> **From WholeChildEducation.org**

In each chapter, I will be detailing easy ways to make this social-emotional connection between coaches and their athletes. Building an emotional connection with each athlete and watching them flourish on and off the field is exactly why I love my job. A coach can have a really significant impact on an athlete. We have the opportunity not only to develop them as a skilled player, but as a better person. It's a huge responsibility but also an incredibly rewarding part of the job.

SUMMARY

- Take a Whole Child Approach when coaching girls.

- Get to know your athletes as people first, players second.

- Girls need a safe and nurturing environment to take risks, allowing them to fully develop as a player.

- Girls need an emotional connection with their coach; they can't be in the unknown.

- Give the girls the first five or ten minutes of practice to let them catch-up; this ensures you have their full attention the rest of the practice.

When you have a girl who is really interested in the sport, don't just shoo her aside because you don't feel that the potential is going to be there. I have girls coming in who want to box, and they are not athletic, and I might initially think that it's not really going to happen. But I've come to never doubt their persistence.

Marc Gargaro, Owner and Trainer, Nonantum Boxing Club

2 ⎢Keeping it Fun

Mia: *It's always the small things that my kids remember about why they loved playing a particular sport or on a particular team. I asked my middle daughter what made her sport teams' experience fun, and she said it was being with friends. And cake. It really made her happy when birthdays were celebrated after practices or games (whatever was closest to the girl's actual birthday), and the parent supplied cupcakes. It's easy to lose sight of the fact that the reason why my child is doing this sport is because it's fun, and the minute it stops being fun, she will move on to something else.*

Alison: Coaches are the first line of defense in making sure that sport is fun for the players. We, as coaches, are driving some of the pressure in sport, and kids are feeling it, whether it's being compared through measurements and statistics, or the drive to be the number one team.

As a coach, it's important to ensure that our athletes aren't feeling overwhelmed by the pressure to get that scholarship, win that trophy, have an undefeated season, be the best.

There is already so much statistical measurement within school. Everything is tested and graded, and it's not healthy for children to feel that they need to win all the time. On top of this, social media amplifies the pressure, with outcomes to games becoming more public, and a greater access to watching and judging the performance of a player online. In this age of testing, measurements and constant sharing, it's easy to lose sight of the fact that the number one reason why kids are playing this sport in the first place is as a release to much of that pressure, and to have fun.

As a coach, it's so important to diffuse some of the pressure in kids' lives. They need to hear that we are here because the sport is fun.

Planning goes a long way into making practices fun. It's important to add lots of variety so that drills don't become tedious, as well as taking into consideration wait times; standing around isn't fun, so think about dividing into smaller groups or setting-up stations for the girls to rotate through to ensure there aren't long lines.

Also consider the varying abilities of your players. I like to design drills where just one person in a group has to hit the goal.

Here's an example of injecting fun into a drill: in every practice, try and involve a skill, like juggling the soccer ball, and then set a goal of 20 juggles. When the first person in each group reaches 20, everyone goes on piggyback to get water. Juggling is a tedious drill, and this turns it from being a stressful, statistical measurement into a team-building and fun exercise.

Note that not everyone has to reach 20 juggles, just one player. This small act of silliness celebrates a group achievement, and everyone will be laughing as they pair-up and piggyback off to their water bottles.

It's a whole different level of stress if you change this drill to say that everyone needs to achieve 20 juggles and the team doesn't move onto the next thing until everyone reaches this mark. "Everyone sit down when you've done your 20 juggles. When everyone is sitting down, we can all go to get water" just doesn't ignite the same enthusiasm, and puts too much pressure on girls who are working to master this skill. Singling them out can trigger them not wanting to come back.

A drill that is designed for fun is a good way to close a practice. Two or three minutes of something silly will leave everyone feeling good as they finish the training session.

Here are more ideas for injecting fun into training:

- Incorporate a relay race, such as a wheelbarrow race or balancing the ball between two heads as you move down the field.

- Arrange a forfeit for the coach if the team or small groups hit a goal, such as 10 push-ups or burpees. The winning team can decide what the coach's forfeit will be.

- Set-up a secret buddy gift exchange at games to enhance team bonding. Reveal the secret buddies at the last game or end of season dinner.

- Arrange pump-up letters which are exchanged before games. Mix the players up so each game has a new pairing. Each player writes a letter or draws a picture about the things they appreciate about that player.

- Set-up a contest with a small reward; it could be as simple as small-sided games with the winners receiving verbal recognition.

- Mix two sports together for a fun drill like Soccer Baseball or Soccer Tennis.

- Give the girls choices; ask them to choose what they want to do or even let them create a drill for the team to undertake.

- Give the team a countdown from five to zero to clean up 50 volleyballs in the gym while coaches try to run off with the balls. The players are never able to achieve clean-up during this period so they then have to do 50 Russian Twists; the situation has been deliberately set-up as a fun way to incorporate core strength drills.

- Play music.

- Verbally recognize Player of the Practice and explain why this person was chosen.

- Set-up stations where the players rotate through different drills; this keeps waiting in line to a minimum.

- Use parents and assistant coaches as passers, rebounders, or ball out-of-bound fetchers to help keep the ball in play longer.

- Make clean-up after the practice a game.

- Celebrate birthdays after practices or games with cupcakes or another treat provided by the parent.

- Recognize improvement and the courage to try something and fail.

- Ask the girls for feedback on whether or not they are having fun, and ask for suggestions on what would make it more enjoyable.

- End practice with the most popular drill.

The reward for always keeping the end goal on having fun is that players will *want* to be at practice. Bearing in mind how busy kids are these days, a sport which has multiple practices throughout the week takes up a great deal of a player's free time and their ability to have playdates. Practice becomes a surrogate playdate.

Players who have fun in their sport end up being players who improve simply because they always show-up, because coming to practice is FUN! Players who love their sport improve, and that in itself supports player development.

SUMMARY

- The number one reason why kids play sports is to have fun.

- The emphasis on having fun should be the dominant goal, not winning.

- Take time to plan practices so that players move quickly from drill to drill with minimum wait time.

- End practice with something designed for fun. It could be a fun drill; it could be recognizing Player of the Practice; it could be cupcakes to celebrate a player's birthday.

- Use games to make tedious drills or exercises more fun.

- Remember to smile! It's always amazing how kids react to adults who smile. Simple but true!

One part of what I try to do as a coach is to provide a space for girls to let their hair down. At the same time, I think it's important to actually want to know what is going on in their lives, and not view them solely as athletes.

Brent Bode, Competitive Novice Girls Head Coach, Community Rowing Inc. (CRI)

In terms of keeping it fun, we give the girls plenty of opportunity to share with each other the things that are going on in their lives. We keep things light; we laugh a lot.

Brent Bode, Competitive Novice Girls Head Coach, Community Rowing Inc. (CRI)

3 | Teaching Growth Mindset

Mia: *I remember the time my daughter was cut from the new club soccer team that had established in our town. She was in fourth grade. All her friends had made the team, but she made 'alternate', which meant she could practice with the team, but couldn't play in games. That situation wasn't going to work for her; she wouldn't thrive on a team that made her feel inferior.*

It was the first time I saw her heart break and it was equally hard for me as a parent. Her town coach was also the new club team coach, and when we declined the 'alternate' spot to take up a place on a different club soccer team, he called. He was upset when he heard that my daughter was heartbroken, and so he offered to talk to her. They chatted and she told him: "You don't think I'm a good player."

Her brave statement would serve to motivate her in the future and also demonstrate that her self-worth wasn't affected. She thought she was good enough to make the team, and that the coach had made a mistake in not picking her.

Growth mindset is exactly that: it's not genetics that makes a good player, it's hard work. And this setback motivated her to put in the work over the next few years to improve. She went on to practice seven days a week until she finally made the top team of her club team.

Fixed Mindset versus Growth Mindset

Alison: Research on Growth Mindset found that the kind of feedback teachers give tends to result in kids either seeking out challenges or taking the easy way out. Feedback which tells kids that they are smart encourages a Fixed Mindset, whereas praising *hard work and effort* fosters a Growth Mindset. When kids have a Growth Mindset, they take on challenges. This in turn, increases their abilities and achievement.

Applying Growth Mindset is simple in theory; don't praise ability or talent, praise hard work and effort. This mindset can be easily applied in sports and supports a development philosophy versus one that is focused solely on winning. For example, in a post-game meeting, the temptation is to recognize the girl who scored the winning goal. But if this was a lazy goal, praise instead the players who worked hard at practice to move the ball from the back, and demonstrated this skill during the game, thus creating the opportunity for the goal.

It's easier said than done. As a coach, the mentality needs to move from winning to development, both at practices and during games. The focus stops being about outcomes, such as game results, but on effort during practice.

Teaching self-advocacy through sports.

Teach important life skills like self-advocacy by letting your child resolve issues by talking directly to the coach without parental interference.

Not only is sports the perfect outlet to teach Growth Mindset, but, if you let girls resolve their issues by talking directly to the coach, it can also impart the important skill of self-advocacy. Encourage parents to allow their child to talk through concerns with their coach such as:

- Getting cut from the team

- Moving up a team
- Not starting
- Playing a different position
- Not enough playing time
- A losing streak
- Depending on age, issues such as schedule conflicts for games or practices and the status of an injury

For coaches, focus on giving feedback that is both constructive and honest. These are some of the things that I say when I have these types of conversations:

- All I ever ask is that you try as hard as you can and be coachable, and I thought you did that.
- This was a great challenge that you took on; you put yourself in a position where you competed with a lot of great players.
- At the end of the day, there are multiple players trying out for the same position. Coaches see different styles of players that they like; this doesn't mean that you aren't a good player, it's completely subjective.
- You need to keep working hard like you did today because coaches value a range of skills and you may make a different team that plays a different style of soccer that better suits your skill set.

Growth Mindset also means a lower team might be the best place for development.

During development years, some players will thrive by going DOWN a level.

Being in the top team should not necessarily be the goal for young players. If your child really loves an activity, it's more important that they find the right environment that allows them to thrive, whether that means a particular coaching style, or a team where they can feel confident and grow. Having fun and wanting to continue the sport is more vital than being on the best team where the child doesn't feel secure.

During the development years, some players will thrive by going DOWN a level; playing on the B-team can provide a more fulfilling experience, because the child feels positive about their abilities, and not as if they are swimming underwater, unable to catch their breath. Going down a level may eventually give that player an enormous boost in confidence.

My advice to parents is to be wary of club teams that have large team rosters. Find out about the club's philosophy towards playing time for non-starters.

If your child is feeling stressed about keeping-up, she may not be on the right team or playing at the right level. For most girls, the feeling of belonging and being valued by their team is more important than the ranking of the team, or the win/loss record. Be aware of the parents who are more caught up in wins and losses than the players, and, if necessary, circle back with parents via email communication about your team philosophy and goals, emphasizing the focus on individual and team development and having fun.

Growth Mindset Teaches Lessons from Failure.

A Growth Mindset attitude in sports focuses on development rather than winning. When faced with 'failure' in the form of losing, go back to the foundation of the qualities you are building. Remind the team that you recognize that they are working hard, and that the team is making progress. Discuss the particular moments of play that you thought were spectacular, even if they didn't result in a goal or a victory. Acknowledge the small improvements so that the players recognize that there is a forward movement.

It's the little things that will translate into a victory.

SUMMARY

- Growth Mindset attitude in sports focuses on development rather than winning.

- Don't praise ability or talent, praise hard work and effort both during practices and games.

- Teach important life skills like self-advocacy by encouraging parents to let their child resolve issues by talking directly to the coach.

- During development years, some players will thrive by going DOWN a level.

Forget Xs and Os, make sure YOU and every coach you surround your players with, teaches each little girl playing the sport that they "CAN DO IT". I have a club team with 600 youth players, and I tell all 40 of my coaches that the goal is to get each little girl a little more confident in herself at each practice. Maybe they don't get better at the sport, but they feel better about themselves so that they will continue to work hard. It will all fall into place at the right time IF and ONLY if she believes in herself. I also think coaches should find a way to teach their young players how to get better in their own time (so that they don't think practice is the only time to improve). Every practice we hold has a section where we teach the players how to work on the skill at home on their own.

Acacia Walker, Head Coach, Women's Lacrosse, Boston College

4 | Building Team Chemistry

Mia: *My oldest daughter played volleyball, and her team would huddle after every point, win or lose. It looked like a very positive thing, girls huddled up, hugging each other. Sometimes it wasn't though. A player in the huddle might assign blame for a lost point, demoralizing the group. Since the coach is not part of the team huddle, the team culture would reveal itself in these moments, good or bad. While the coach can't control what happens in the huddle, it's an extension of the team culture created during practices. It's a little like baking bread; you need all the right ingredients at the right temperature. If you do all the right things and create the right environment, the bread rises on its own.*

Alison: One of my daughter's teammates was invited to attend a national training camp. The coach told the players to kick the ball around in small groups before practice started. She approached a group and asked if she could join. A girl asked if she had been to this camp before.

"No, this is my first time," she replied.

"This group is only for girls who have been to camp multiple times."

The coach may not have realized what just happened, but this type of experience can make girls devalue themselves and lose their confidence. It's definitely not the kind of chemistry that promotes teamwork. While a coach may not be aware of every conversation that happens, creating a team atmosphere of inclusiveness starts at the top. A coach needs to communicate what is important to him or her, and the team will follow this lead.

It's the coach's job to teach equal value of all players in their organization.

It's the coach's job to teach equal value of all players. Something as minor as forming small groups can promote cliques (see Chapter Twelve). Coaches can combat exclusion by counting off or assigning the groups during practices.

The coach should also be cognizant of who is recognized, whether it's to demonstrate a particular skill or be the team captain. It's really important to rotate as evenly as possible so as not to signal favoritism.

I like to create a culture of team-building by creating traditions that help to institutionalize it. I begin by making sure our freshman feel an equal part of the team. I assign an upper classmen to each freshman in a Big Sister - Little Sister program. They help the freshmen buy their books and take them to their classes during the first week of school, and establish a bond even before the freshmen arrive at college.

However, it goes beyond just orientation. Our team knows that when we sit down to a team dinner, the six spots at each table need to be filled by a freshman, sophomore, junior and senior, with the last two spots for any year. Even though I usually don't have to specify this, this applies also to practices when we form small groups.

We also have Maroon and Gold Team match up, reflecting our school colors. My assistant coaches hold a draft – no trades are allowed – and each assistant leads a team. This builds a bond between the players and the assistant coaches. Each team even has their own personalized cheer.

We keep a big board in the locker room to record the Maroon and Gold competitions. Every player is included and points for your team can be won through one v one shooting or scrimmages. However, earning points for your team is not just based on skills; points are also awarded for the highest GPA, as well as trivia contests on the bus on the 'History of Our Program', or '10 Questions on the Opponent'. It gives the chance for every member of the team to contribute.

By awarding points to non-sports related skills, a sense of equality is created. A player who rarely gets playing time during a game can still gain points for her team. We also include points for fitness and community service, areas where players who are the least skilled can still gain recognition. I've noticed that the strongest players often compliment the weaker players when they are awarded points, and that helps to make everyone feel valued, improving team chemistry.

The huddle talk is a good indication of team chemistry.

You can see the team chemistry at play during a setback in a game. Are the players giving each other positive messages? Are they holding their heads up? What is the energy level? Is it going up or down? By noticing your team's chemistry on the field, you can give recognition to the behavior of players during the post-game meeting in order to reinforce teamwork. This signals to your players what is important to you.

Team building for youth sports.

For youth sports, institutionalizing team building can be a few easy activities like:

- Playing the 'How to Be a Good Teammate' game (see Chapter Five).

- Create a Team Captain schedule before the season begins (see Chapter Thirteen).

- Control the small groups by counting off.

- Recognize Player of The Practice for each practice, highlighting the characteristics of hard work and determination, as opposed to skill based qualities. Giving this verbal award to new players on the team early in the season signals their value to the team.

- Specify criteria for forming small groups, for instance, find a partner who you don't go to school with, who lives in a different town, or who you've never played with previously.

- Recognize contributions/assists that lead up to scoring instead of just the player who scored the goal.

- Praise behavior that builds teamwork such as the player who cleaned up the field without anyone asking, or who gave a positive message to the team in the huddle after a setback.

- Give the players ten minutes to socialize at the beginning of practice so they can strengthen their relationships with each other.

- Recognize effort instead of outcomes.

SUMMARY

- Team culture is established at the top by the coach.
- Take active steps to build team chemistry: give every player a chance to be team captain, assign or count off for small groups, recognize hard work and not just skill.
- Use the verbal award of Player of the Practice to reinforce behavior that builds team chemistry such as hard work, supportive attitude, or a new player who joined the team.
- Use games such as 'How to Be a Good Teammate' (see Chapter Five) to reinforce team chemistry and make practices fun.

Don't underestimate how competitive girls can be and how much they want to learn. I found that the more competitive I would make practice, the more enjoyable and the more intense and invested the players would be. Girls love to compete.

Sarah Dacey, Head Coach of Women's Soccer, Barry University

Communication is also very important. Girls are people pleasers by nature so they want to feel like they are doing right by their coaches and they want to work hard. Positive reinforcement and encouragement are essential. At the end of the day, the players want to have 'fun' but as coaches it is our responsibility to still teach the game the right way. There is no reason why coaches can't make sessions enjoyable and allow the players to learn at the same time. Finding that balance is key.

Sarah Dacey, Head Coach of Women's Soccer, Barry University

My best advice to a girls' youth coach is to focus on the culture of the team. If you emphasize and teach body language, eye contact, hustle, togetherness, energy, attitude, responsibility, communication, focus, etc. then EVERYTHING else you teach about your sport will be better. These are also the skills that your players will need in school and in life. Sports and 'real life' mirror each other as they reward those who display those characteristics.

Erik Johnson, Head Coach of Women's Basketball, Boston College

5 The 'How to Be a Good Teammate' game

Mia: *I love how this game combines teaching kids in a concrete and physical way how to be a good teammate but is also really entertaining. It's essentially a version of freeze tag. It can be modified for any sport, and changed-up to become a technical drill. An added bonus is that it teaches kids to look up and really see the field. By identifying who is in trouble, this game is a defensive drill that teaches doubling down. Use it as a fun way to end practice!*

This game builds teamwork and is hilariously fun.

Note that it is not about winning, and there's no score!

Alison: Count the team off in 10's and put the evens on one side and the odds on the other. You want approximately 10 players per side, but it's easy to modify for a larger or smaller number.

With 10 players per side, you will need three pinnies (vest) and 3 balls. You can use any kind of ball. The primary way to play this game is to throw and catch the ball, therefore a nerf football works well, but you can also use the ball of the sport the athletes play, such as a soccer ball, basketball, or lacrosse ball.

Give three pinnies to the team with the even numbers, and three balls to the odd number side. If you have a ball, you are 'safe'. The girls with the pinnies in their hands need to tag those on the other team who don't have a ball by touching them with a pinnie; that player will then be unable to move. To 'unfreeze' a player, she needs to be thrown a ball by one of her teammates. When she catches the ball, she is then free to move. Now, she has the ball and can look around the field to spot a player on her team in trouble (i.e. being chased by an opponent with a pinnie), and throw that player the ball to give her immunity.

Note that there are no winners or losers in this game, just frozen or unfrozen players. There is also no point scoring. There's a reason for that; this game is not about winning, it's about noticing and helping a member of your team who is in trouble, thus being a good teammate.

If you have more than 10 players per side, add one pinnie and one ball for every two additional players per side. Alternately, subtract a pinnie and ball for every two players less than 10.

The point of this game is teaching players to be a good teammate by noticing who needs help.

Your athletes might see this only as a fun game, but what they are actually doing is:

- Seeing the field
- Noticing who is in trouble
- Helping a teammate
- Making quick decisions while in motion

This game also works as a defensive team building drill to teach doubling down. It trains players to recognize when a teammate needs help, and give them support by doubling down on the opponent.

Switch this game to a technical drill by dribbling and passing the ball on the ground instead of throwing and catching it.

You can easily switch this game into a technical drill by placing the soccer ball on the ground. Now, instead of throwing the ball, it's a dribble and passing drill.

If you want to use this game to end every practice but want to increase the level of difficulty, try switching out the ball. Instead of using the standard soccer ball, use the small one. Or try with a tennis ball. Whether the ball is thrown and caught, or dribbled and passed, using different sized balls that the team are not used to working with makes this drill fun and challenging for every player.

SUMMARY

- The 'How to Be a Good Teammate' game is a version of freeze tag.
- It teaches players to have field vision and to spot teammates in trouble and provide assistance.
- Players think this game is fun but it also teaches them defensive doubling down.
- Change up the balls to make this game more challenging.
- This can also be a technical drill by dribbling and passing instead of throwing and catching.

6 | Positive Reinforcement is Critical

Mia: *My daughter's club volleyball coach is amazing; he thanks players for running for an out of bounds ball that they have no hope of getting. They would walk through fire for him. I asked him when we headed over to the team dinner one night if he had always coached this way. He told me that he used to be the kind of coach who was the hardest on the most promising player, but he learned that you can't coach girls in that way.*

Alison: Girls want to be pushed but they need positive reinforcement. It's important for them to feel that even when you're pushing them, you still believe in them. Which means that you can't just give them positive feedback at the end of practice, they need a small amount of positive reinforcement throughout practice.

A female player can't be in the unknown.

A female player can't be in the unknown, she needs to be sure that her coach thinks she is good enough. You can't assume that because she scored five goals in the small-sided game that she knows that she had a good training session.

I saw this in evidence just recently in training; girls can really improve during practice if you encourage them. When they achieve something that you have been asking of them, giving them a quick boost with some praise can go a long way. Never assume that they know that they are doing well, it's rarely the case.

Once you've noticed a player has done something positive, compliment it right away. A player will grow from that.

For example, Helena* was stripped of the ball three times in practice. She needed to look over her shoulder to see pressure. As soon as she did that, BOOM! My feedback to her was: "That's exactly the turn that I need you to do.

Girls need to trust you

You turned away from pressure really well." And she didn't lose the ball in the midfield throughout the rest of practice!

What you can't say is: "Stop losing the ball!" A response along those lines will usually result in her then losing the ball for the rest of training. As soon as she masters the skill that you wanted her to work on – it doesn't have to result in a goal, it's that she turned, escaped pressure, and connected a ball – you need to praise it straightaway. In my experience, she'll then demonstrate that skill again and again.

There are certain girls on the team to whom I could say regarding a forty-yard pass: "Come on, Jo Jo*, you have to connect that out of the back." We've built a relationship on trust, so I can send her that message in the knowledge that she knows I still value her as a player.

However, I couldn't say that to a freshman who isn't as sure about her standing in the team. I would have to be more positive. She has to know that I am there for her, that I do believe in her, and that I think that she's a good player. Once she trusts me, I can give a little bit more. I could eventually say: "That's the one that we can't lose in the back", knowing that it wouldn't erode her confidence.

SUMMARY

- Girls need to know that you, as the coach, believe in them.

- While girls need constant feedback during practice, it needs to always be positive until a trusting relationship is established.

- Once you notice a player has done something positive, compliment it right away.

- Give this constant stream of positive feedback to everyone on the team, as evenly as possible.

I spend 80% of my time in a clinic with the lower group kids and that's been the key to retention. As elite coaches, our affinity is to go to that top group. What I've learned in managing clinics is that I'll put the top kids in one group and find a couple leaders that can run the drills for me. That's a tremendous lesson to me. They are very peer motivated at that time and they are practicing leadership skills. I've taught myself to go to the second and third tier group and spend most of my coaching energy there. That's allowed me to get that retention. The top tier is coming back because they are already in a position where they are motivated to learn the sport. It's that lower group kids that I want to make sure that they have the confidence where they want to come back the next day.

Ainslee Lamb, Natick Middle School Coach and National Team Coach for USA Women's Field Hockey

The relationship between coach and player can take one of two forms: it either allows a player to flourish, get better at the game, but more importantly learn to love the game, or the coach can constantly yell, denigrate, and point out faults in players. I believe the most successful teams out there are the ones who are constantly telling their players, using positive feedback, what they need to do versus what they don't need to do. That helps immensely in allowing someone, young or old, to accept constructive criticism. We have seen the change come for some time now. There are many college coaches being fired because of the denigrating way in which they act towards their players to get them to excel. If we talk to our players in a way that promotes positive actions, people tend to play much better and they want to play harder. And that's across the board for any sport, not just volleyball.

Fabian (Fabe) Ardila, President at MGA Sports Inc., and High Performance Court Coach, USA Volleyball

names changed to protect player's identity.

7 Developing Good People, Not Just Good Players

Mia: *My kids probably respected and sometimes even feared their coach more than any other authority figure in their lives. He or she was the person whose opinion they worried about the most: does my coach like me? Am I going to start?*

Coaches can use this influence in a variety of really positive ways. I noticed that my middle daughter's town coach would work with her team on kindness and appreciating every member of the team through pump-up letters before games. In both small and big ways, coaches have an enormous influence that can be tapped and used to encourage athletes to develop not just as good players, but good people.

Alison: The role of the coach can influence far beyond the field, and that's why it's important to recognize the significance of qualities unrelated to the sport that can help develop players into good people. For example, I coach U14 girls on a club team and I might recognize a player for being courteous because they let someone cut in front of them in line; they saw that a player didn't have a chance to take a turn, so they let them go ahead, as opposed to having the attitude of 'I am going to be the first one in front of the college coach who's recruiting here today'.

"Round of applause for Miriam for being courteous. She let Jocelyn go ahead of her."

"Round of applause for Adriana for collecting balls at the end of practice. That's really nice."

"Round of applause for Jackie who did a slide tackle and sacrificed her body for the team."

"A round of applause for Serena who was the first over when there was an injury on the field. She forgot about the ball and just ran over to check on her teammate. You're the player of the day!"

I think we should be encouraging our athletes to develop qualities through sports that really matter in life, like helping others out, and being thoughtful and courteous. Unless I compliment that behavior, my players will never know that it's important to me as a coach.

> *We need to let players understand that other things are important besides winning and getting drafted, such as being kind and caring about others.*

Here's an example of what happened in practice recently. We had two girls who went to New Orleans for ten days during break to help build homes. They stayed in dorms, got up early, and worked all day, and even into the night. We also had two players who got drafted to play soccer professionally. We opened-up our team meeting with an appreciation of the two girls who just did something phenomenal the previous week.

> *We talked about the girls who volunteered their time.*

And this communicated to my team the qualities that their coach prioritizes.

This is not to say that it wasn't also phenomenal that two players were chosen to play professionally. Playing professionally though isn't an opportunity that all my players will have, but we all have the ability to give back to our community.

If you get your athletes to understand – and maybe these are not the ones who will play professionally – that the other things they do with their time also matters, they will work tirelessly for you. They will find a way.

If you only talk about getting drafted, you lose 95% of your audience.

Player of the day doesn't have to go to the leading scorer. This translates to youth soccer too. The power of youth coaching is that we, as coaches, are in great positions to teach lessons at any age. We can shift priorities and still win.

For example, there might be one kid on your team who is going to score all the goals. If you have an award for leading scorer during practices and games, it's likely that it will go to the same one or two girls. It's easy to give praise to the girl who is the best, but recognize that you are putting them on an island. Nine times out of ten, the girl in question doesn't want that.

However, the award for courteousness, helping-out, being unselfish, or seeing that someone on the other team is hurt and going over to help her, these are areas of recognition that everyone has the opportunity to receive. Those players who might not win recognition for scoring goals will improve because they will take more chances for you. They grow to know that "coach believes in me. Coach knows who I am and what I'm all about." And that's essential in building the trust relationship between me as the coach and her as my player.

SUMMARY

- Recognize non-sports related activities to let players know that coach thinks being courteous and kind are equally important as winning.

- Always recognizing the most skilled player may not be what that player wants, and might be socially isolating for her with her teammates.

- Verbal recognition, such as asking for a round of applause for great behavior also helps build a trust relationship with players.

- If only skill based achievements are recognized, this generally goes to the same small group and leaves the rest of the team out.

- Athletes will feel that you understand them and value them for non-sports related things, and as a result, they will work harder for you, making them better players.

The best team building exercise I use in my program happens right after the holidays. I ask each player to spend a few days during that time forming their legacy. I ask them to consider what they want to be remembered for after they graduate. I purposely emphasize that their legacy should not be solely based on statistics and awards. Instead, they should include how they want to be remembered as people.

- Do they want to be remembered for being a difference maker in a person's life or do they want to be remembered as the teammate who showed up to practice every single day with a smile on her face and the look of pure determination in her eyes?

- Do they want to be remembered as the teammate who had their back?

- Or do they want to be remembered as the friend who would always lend an ear?

This team building exercise can be implemented with today's youth to promote the importance of being a good teammate and person, which in turn will create future leaders and captains.

Ashley Obrest, Head Softball Coach, Boston College

8 | Social Awareness and Giving Back to the Community

Mia: *My girls' club soccer team holds an annual soccer charity event whereby the entire club plays soccer for twenty-four hours straight. Each age level is assigned a two-hour block of time where they scrimmage against the boys' teams with music pumping in the background. The coaches jump in and play too, which makes it especially fun for the teams. Each player is asked to raise $400 towards soccer scholarships and the Special Olympics. It's a great way for the kids to channel their love of soccer towards a social cause, and it allows them a chance to interact with other teams in the club who they wouldn't otherwise see.*

Alison: We have the opportunity as coaches to educate beyond the game, by encouraging our players to give back outside the sport. If we take part in a community service project, our team has the chance to learn that there are kids in Kenya who play soccer barefoot because they don't own cleats or who don't have running water in their houses. At the same time, it's also a way to improve team chemistry, by coming together to give back.

Community service can also serve to decrease bullying by teaching kids a greater sense of empathy and understanding towards other people's situations. Sometimes the girls are so busy that if we don't offer this opportunity, it's hard for them to find the time to take part in charitable activities. It's positive for the club too, moving away from the pattern of focusing solely on player improvement, and instead, sending constructive messages to the team about kindness.

It's your responsibility as a coach to prove that it's about more than just wins and losses. Greatness isn't just about victories; it's about helping others and making a difference where possible.

You have to prove as a coach that it's about more than just wins and losses.

The bigger message is that some days we win, some days we lose, but that we are highly fortunate to be in the position of being able to give back. This valuable life lesson will hopefully influence a young person's perspective on what really matters.

We already have the organization, in the form of our team, to work together to help others. Scheduling the project during a practice ensures that everyone can make it, and demonstrates that the coach values this experience as much as player development. A service project also creates opportunities for leadership to those players who perhaps are not the most skilled on the field. Ideas for service projects within your community can include:

- Organizing a used athletic shoe/cleat/uniform drive.
- Junior Coach program where older players (e.g. U16) help younger teams (e.g. U9) during a practice.
- Older players can mentor younger kids by helping them with homework or reading with them. This could be a younger team from your town or club. Set up a space on a common field or in a room at a practice facility.
- Ask the team to create a gentle exercise class at a local nursing or assisted living home which they can then do with the residents.
- Ask a special needs child from your community, who may play an adaptive form of the sport, if they would like to join for a

practice, and let your players plan a practice around including him or her.

- Plan a fundraising activity for a cause close to the hearts of your players; perhaps there is a parent/guardian/sibling who is battling a serious disease. The activity can either be related to a specific skill for that sport with pledges for how long a player juggles a soccer ball, or can be more general, such as a car wash or bake sale.

- Hold a sports clinic for younger girls as a fundraiser.

At Boston College, our girls' soccer team volunteers for team IMPACT (www.goteamimpact.org). I invite my players who don't get as much playing time to join me on team IMPACT individually. These players might not play in games, and therefore, I don't have game tape to review with them. Team IMPACT gives them the same opportunity to meet with me. This also lets them know that I value them even if they don't get playing time.

I designate three of the players on team IMPACT as my leadership team. Together, we decide what we want to accomplish. In years past, we have 'adopted' a girl with Cerebral Palsy who plays adaptive soccer. Our team IMPACT thought about the little things; they organized for her to hang out with a smaller portion of the team so that meeting the entire team would not be overwhelming for her. They asked her to join them in the locker room where they had a locker and game jersey with her name on it. She also participated with the team during practices and pregame warm-ups.

We have also held a fundraiser for a young local soccer player, Ashley Baird, who was diagnosed with a rare form of cancer when she was in Junior High School. Our team decided on a soccer ball juggling fundraiser because she loves to juggle. The money raised went to help fund childhood cancer research for her specific kind of cancer. Because her number is 12, we solicited friends and family to sponsor players for $12 for half an hour of juggling.

We have a player on our team whose father died of Lou Gehrig's disease. We hold an annual fundraiser for this cause at one of our games by organizing a silent auction of soccer balls signed by our team.

My team also volunteers their time by putting on free soccer clinics for the local girls' town soccer teams. We promote the fun of the game and it gives my players a chance to connect with younger girls. The players who shine at this are not necessarily my starting line-up, and it provides another opportunity for me as the coach to celebrate their contributions as mentors and leaders.

I have players recovering from long term injuries who are literally unable to play for months, and who think their lives are over. I have found that adding them to our social awareness committee, team IMPACT, is as important for their rehabilitation as physical therapy. Emotionally, it gives them a broader perspective, and an outlet for contributing. Helping others is a highly uplifting experience, and serves as a beacon that can help my graduates find their way as they leave college and start to think about their careers.

The benefits of teaching players social awareness lasts a lifetime. It gives kids who might be stressed out by normal, everyday life a valuable perspective. It also provides my players with concrete proof that I am not totally focused on the final result of games. Finally, it serves as a team bonding experience that makes us all feel good.

SUMMARY

- Creating a community service project for a team or a sports club gives athletes who might not have time to give back an opportunity to participate.

- Players have concrete evidence that the coach is not solely focused on wins and losses by organizing a community service team project.

- Giving back presents the team with a broader perspective that can be a life changing experience.

- A social awareness project can build team chemistry and allows other members on the team to shine.

- Social awareness projects can be tied to community members such as loved ones battling illnesses.

- For players who face long recovery time from injuries, it helps them to stay connected to the team, and gives them something positive to focus on.

- Please see our resource list on our website (howtocoachgirls. com) of sports related non-profit organizations if you are looking for ideas for social awareness projects for your team. Thank you for emailing us with suggestions for this list (pragmaticmomblog@gmail.com).

THE BIG PICTURE – *NOTES*

SOLUTIONS TO SPECIFIC ISSUES

SOLUTIONS TO SPECIFIC ISSUES

9 | Coaching Your Own Daughter

Mia: *My husband coached all of our kids for soccer at various levels, from kindergarten soccer to our oldest's U13 team, where he ran a weekly practice session. It was harder for him to coach girls as they became tweens. He felt that the girls tended to waste time talking amongst themselves, and didn't seem to take the sport seriously enough. That put pressure on our daughter to be the 'good example' which she did not enjoy. On the other hand, my husband felt he was volunteering specifically for her because the team had a coaching crisis. While they worked through their challenges as the season unfolded, it would have been helpful for my husband and daughter to address these issues before they stepped on the pitch.*

Alison: Coaching your own daughter can be tricky. I've found the best way to handle conflicts that arise when a parent is also a coach is to talk about it before the season begins.

Step 1: Accepting Your Parent in the Coaching Role

The immediate reaction of my daughter when she learns that I am volunteering to assist coach her team is generally not one of enthusiasm. One way I position my role is to let her know that parents are helping the team in a number of different ways because of their skill sets and that this is my way of contributing. Parents who are good at computer skills are helping behind the scenes by organizing carpools and snacks, ordering uniforms, or running the team communications. My daughter may not have realized that other parents assist the team because their roles are not as visible. Once my daughter became aware that other parents are also volunteering, and that running practices is my strength, she was more willing to accept me in this role.

> For that hour and half, you are everyone's coach, and your child has to be treated equally. I'm asking her for equal feedback and I'm asking her to respond like all the other kids.

Step 2: Coach versus Parent

Before I can accept the role of Assistant Coach, I need to have a conversation with my daughter about changing our relationship for that hour and a half when I am coaching. We both have to be comfortable with a different dynamic during that time period to create an environment of equality.

That hour and a half is going to feel different even though I love her more than everybody else; but as the coach, my goal is to treat everyone equally. I ask her to be respectful of me as she would a teacher, and we decide on how we will handle conflict resolution for the instances that she does not like what I am doing.

It's important that she understands that I'm striving for fairness towards all members of the team. Making sure that my daughter is treated impartially will also circumvent possible resentment from girls on the team that the coach's daughter gets 'favored status'. That being said, it's also easy to go in the opposite direction, and unnecessarily penalize your own daughter to avoid a perception of favoritism.

The coach versus parent conversation can start with girls as young as aged five.

Here are some ideas on what to discuss:

- How is your daughter going to communicate when she doesn't like something that you are doing? Agree on a process for getting her feedback during practices. Instead of telling you during practice: "Nobody wants to dribble the ball through cones right now", have a designated time when she can privately share her assessment of the practice.

- Assure her that you are going to treat all the players equally in terms of playing time and recognition which doesn't mean that you don't love her any less when you are the coach.

- Give her a task that she excels in that will help you out on the team. For example, if she has leadership qualities, she can help you get players back from water breaks and ready to go. Find a role that suits her so that she has a positive reward for her parent coaching the team.

- Let her know that as a player, she doesn't get input into decisions about who is starting, or even access to this information ahead of time.

Some Pitfalls to Avoid:

- **Surprising your daughter that you are the coach:** Getting her acceptance before the season begins is key to a smooth start. If you don't have those conversations about your role, you'll end up fielding problems at the same time as you are coaching.

- **Positive feedback to players:** It's important to give regular, positive feedback to all players, but there might be one person on the team with whom your daughter feels particularly competitive. Feedback to that person might make her react adversely. In this case, just ensure that you haven't given less feedback to your own child in an effort to seem impartial. Coupling feedback to both of them might be a good strategy. Realize that it's difficult for your daughter to watch you give attention to other players and that she might not be able to verbalize this to you. Instead she may behave badly.

- **Spotlighting players:** Let your daughter know that although there will be times when you will ask her to demonstrate, you will be rotating this role among the players. The role of captain and co-captains will also rotate evenly, preferably in a schedule that is determined and communicated before the season begins.

- **When mom is coach:** Developmentally, tween girls start to define their own identity through their differences with their mother. As a result, it can be more challenging for moms than dads to coach their daughters.

- **Cries for attention:** If your daughter is quietly messing around in a cry for attention, ignore it if it's not disruptive to the team. Instead, compliment someone else who is doing a good job. When your daughter comes around, compliment her then.

- **Limited influence:** Your daughter, even though she might have strong opinions as to who should play a certain position or be in the starting line-up, has no influence on these types of coaching decisions. Don't let her think she has authority because she happens to be the coach's daughter.

- **Car ride home:** Change your mode from coach to mom on the car ride home. Don't bring up the game except in the broadest, most complimentary way. This isn't the time to tell her what she could have done during the game to be a better player.

In the car ride home, switch back to parent mode.
Don't address their performance or behavior right then.
Perhaps you have a preset time to give each other
feedback, post practice or game.

This is a lengthy conversation to have with your daughter and might indeed be a series of conversations. The important thing is that your daughter feels as if her objections to her parent taking on the role have been heard. Equally important is that once her approval has been given, the different scenarios for possible conflicts are discussed. This will make the season go much more smoothly for both of you.

SUMMARY

- Before a parent agrees to be a coach or assistant coach, talk to your daughter and get her approval.

- Have conversations with your daughter about how being her coach will feel different from being her parent for that hour and a half.

- Go over potential conflicts, and work out how your daughter can give feedback in a constructive way off the field.

- Find a positive for your daughter – a special role for helping you – as the coach's daughter.

- Be mindful of giving attention evenly, but be careful not

to under compliment your daughter in an effort to appear fair. There may be times when she needs some recognition to cope with sharing you with her teammates.

One of the things that I really made sure of is to treat my daughter fairly and with equity with regard to her teammates. I did work really hard to make sure that there was an end to the practice or the game, that it didn't then carry on to dinner or after dinner. I really tried to compartmentalize what our relationship was with me coaching her on the field, and then really made sure I was her mom the rest of the time. And vice versa too, I wanted her to make sure that while we were on the field, it really was a coach/player relationship. I think I was able to do that though because I emphasized having a positive experience, having fun, encouraging her to enjoy the environment she was in. There were no expectations of performance, or winning or losing.

I also felt it was very important that I didn't have conversations with her beyond I would have anyone else on the team. I wasn't going to talk to her friend about what did you think of my daughter's performance today? I would never put her in that same position of asking her who do you think was the best player today unless I was going to have that conversation with everyone on the team. It helped me to compartmentalize those roles. I wanted to be both her coach and her mom but I had to realize that I couldn't be both at the same time.

Ainslee Lamb, Natick Middle School Coach and National Team Coach for USA Women's Field Hockey

I can tell you about my experience with my kids. I didn't want anyone in the world to feel that there was any nepotism, that I was favoring my kids over anybody else. In avoiding this, I was tougher on my own kids. Everyone else got treated the same, but I was always a little tougher on my own daughters to show that they didn't get special treatment. My advice to parents who are coaching on their daughter's team is not to treat your child any differently from the way you treat anyone else on the team. Make sure you aren't babying anyone, especially your child, and don't make excuses for your kid. Do have the right relationship with all the players including your child and make sure you treat them equally. That goes a long way when you communicate to the group. In treating everyone the same, you will get the respect of the group.

Fabian (Fabe) Ardila, President at MGA Sports Inc., and High Performance Court Coach, USA Volleyball

10 | Playing Time

Mia: *I've experienced two kinds of playing-time issues with my middle daughter. When she was in kindergarten soccer, she would not play at all if I was near the field. Instead, she would want to sit on my lap. I was banned by the coach and my husband for most of the season in order to get my daughter to play! As she became older and played club soccer, she was very cognizant of playing time. Starting and playing time was a proxy for the social pecking order of the team. It's this perceived relationship of starting/playing time and social status on the team that coaches should be aware of. Even mixing up the starting line-up once a season signals to the players that everyone is valued, and that there are no 'favorites'.*

Alison: It's important for the coach to give a pre-season message about playing time and starting philosophy. I believe that for U12 teams and younger, every player should have equal starting and playing time. They should also play different positions, and everyone should have the opportunity to sit on the bench.

For very young players, coaches may have a different kind of problem concerning participation. Some kids might not want to play at all during games! Taking a very gentle approach to young athletes is important. I found that asking them if a friend or sibling holding their hand on the field would help. Much of the time it does.

> Coaches should look for games where the line-up can be switched up so that everyone gets a chance to start.

Stating a clear message about playing and starting time also preempts concerns that the coach's daughter may get favored status. Creating a line-up ahead of time, including a rotation schedule, will help ensure that playing time is equal during games.

For older girls playing at the U15 age group, playing time and the starting line-up is more likely to be based on the player's ability; but even for older teams, coaches should look for games with a weaker opponent where the line-up can be switched around so that everyone gets a chance to start the game.

Coaches run into problems when they don't define their playing time expectation or philosophy to players and parents before the season begins. If it's a high level of competition and you, as the coach, want to start the best players and give them more playing time, you must state that at the very start to avoid any misunderstandings. There should be no surprises.

> Players on the bench should be engaged and supportive of their teammates on the field. When starters sit on the bench, it is their opportunity to reciprocate the support given to them all year.

Coaches should also articulate their philosophy concerning the attitude of players on the bench. To enhance team chemistry, I expect players who are sitting out to be engaged in the game and supportive of their team mates on the field.

When my leading players sit on the bench, I see this as their opportunity to reciprocate the support that has been given to them all year. It is their chance to appreciate when their teammates do something well. By rotating my starting line-up when possible, for example in pre-season games, I can give all my players this same chance.

It may seem like a small thing, but a coach can build team chemistry by preventing players from demonstrating negative body language on the bench, either because they are unhappy with their playing time or the way in which they've played. It allows them to think about the other members of the group rather than be focused on themselves.

If I can teach my players to appreciate the support from the bench from those who receive less playing time, they are more likely to reciprocate support when we focus on other ways of contributing to the team, for example, during our social awareness 'giving-back' project. It encourages them to be vocal in their encouragement when we recognize other accomplishments during locker room meetings, such as a player's G.P.A., or their various extracurricular activities. Making every player feel valued by both the coach and their teammates is the crux of team chemistry. It's something that we work on every day, all year.

SUMMARY

- Give a clear pre-season message about playing and starting philosophy.

- For U12 players and younger, everyone should have equal playing time, equal starting time, and play all the positions.

- For very young players who don't want to participate, try having siblings or friends take them on the field during games.

- For older girls, playing time and the starting line-up could change based on their ability. In that case, look for opportunities to switch the starting line-up.

- Players on the bench need to be engaged and supportive of their teammates.

- When leading players are on the bench, it is their opportunity to reciprocate the support they have received all season.

11 | Building a Player's Confidence

Mia: *I've noticed that every time my daughters' come into something new, whether it's a new team or a new sport, there's a period of adjustment and of finding their place in the pecking order. During this assessment period, they aren't feeling very confident. They rely on signals from their coach and teammates to relay to them that they are valued and that they are 'good'. It's an uncomfortable place of insecurity, of being judged, and of not having trusted relationships with everyone. It doesn't matter if it's an individual sport or a team sport, I've noticed. For every new beginning, a player needs support to build her confidence.*

Alison: There are some crucial fundamentals to establish to help build a player's confidence. The first step is the culture that you create. It's essential to create a culture of safety. I, as your coach, can't help you with your confidence level if you are looking over your shoulder thinking that you might be cut. First and foremost is making every player feel secure.

How do you, as the coach, create this?

Trust is Number One.

It starts with trust and establishing a relationship with each player based on her as a whole person, not just her skills as an athlete.

Loyalty is Number Two.

Loyalty from the coach to the player is the next step. Each player needs to feel that the coach is loyal to her and that she is not in danger of getting cut. "I'm going to say some tough things to you at times but you have my loyalty. I'm not kicking you out."

It's crucial to create a culture of safety before you can help a player build confidence.

Girls need a whole person approach to relationships. They need to feel that you value them as a person, not just a player. Having dialogue with your players is more powerful than discussion because it implies listening. There are different approaches, for example, to telling a player that she won't start.

A dialogue approach would be:

"We talked about what to work on these past few weeks and I see that you're working hard on this. I think right now, with the combination of people we have, we need a different skill set to get to where we want to be with this team. We're not giving up on you. You have improved. We want to keep working with you, but right now we are going to start someone else in that position, but with your improvement, we are going to need you to come right off that bench and help out."

Everyone wants to be needed, so how do you tell the non-starter that she's needed?

"As the energy goes down in that game, we are going to need all your hard work to get out there with everything that you've been working on to make a difference. Because that's when the game is going to be changed; when you get out there. And I've seen it in your training. I've seen how much you've worked. Starting now or not starting, we don't want to make that the priority; but when you get in that game, that's the moment to use the 1v1 skills that you've worked so hard on to beat her inside, and I know that you are going to be able to get that done in the game."

It still might not be what they wanted to hear. They most likely wanted to be in that starting line-up, but if you have a safe environment where they trust and respect you, you are still complimenting their performance. You are recognizing how hard they work and that their final touch to get past a defender has improved so that when they get out on the field, they will make a difference. It might not be in the first twenty minutes of the game, but it's the next twenty minutes when I put her in that we really need the game changer.

These are actual conversations that I have with my players and it's the truth. Sometimes the moment of most impact in a game is not at the start, and I really do want the best player to come in midway to change the momentum of the game.

A harder conversation is with a player who won't be getting any playing time. It takes a different approach to make her feel valued. I'll recognize her for her work off the field. The community service that we do as a team and her role in it as an exceptional representative who is able to relate to the kids, and make a difference in a child's life. Academically, she also makes an important contribution to the team. Professors of hers will tell me what a great student she is and I'll let her know that she makes me feel very proud, and that she helped to boost the team G.P.A. There are so many different ways to contribute to a team. I want her to know that I don't evaluate her as a person based on her playing time or how many goals she scored. It goes back to creating good people and not just good players.

SUMMARY

- Building a player's confidence starts with creating a culture of safety.

- Each player needs to know that the coach is loyal and committed to her and that they are in no danger of being cut.

- After a safe culture has been established, helping players with their confidence level is a process of setting goals, and getting constant feedback from the coach.

- Coaches can give tough feedback if the relationship with their player is based on mutual trust and respect.

- Having dialogue versus discussion is an important way to keep the communication two-way.

- Recognize a player's improvement and hard work.

Understand your players. Some players may need more positive reinforcement than others. Sometimes those players may even need you to say "great pass" even if it was a 15 yard pass completed under pressure. Make sure you understand that isn't praising a player for making a mistake. This is helping a player build confidence.

There are also times when you need to be hard/demanding on a player. They want to know what they are doing wrong and how to fix it. Just yelling at a player telling them what they already know doesn't help a player develop. These kids are human and will make mistakes, but they need to understand that at the next level making continuous mistakes may cause them limited playing time.

I tell my players I am their biggest fan but I am hard and I am demanding. I want to help develop them into the best player that they can be and help them follow their goals and dreams and the goals of the team.

Mary-Frances Monroe, Head Coach of Women's Soccer, University of Miami

I would say to empower young girls. They need to let them know it's OK to be the best and to strive to be the best. I think sometimes young girls don't want to stand out from the crowd and the coaches need to give them the confidence to do so.

Amanda Cromwell, Head Soccer Coach, Women's Soccer, UCLA

12 | Cliques on and off the field

Mia: *An issue for my middle daughter when she played club soccer was carpools. The problem was that she was the only person on her team from her town. There were three other carpools based on location and then a few girls who were also the only ones from their town. It wasn't that the girls from town carpools were inherently mean or exclusive or catty … but they came into practice as group who carpooled together, and most had played together for years on town teams together. They talked about people who went to their school who no one else knew. And, on the field, one group had a – most likely unconscious – tendency to pass to each other.*

Alison: If you tell girls to form teams of four, they will naturally go into groups based on who they know socially. It may be a group of girls from the same town who carpool together. The group may be from the same elementary school if it's a town team. It may be by age group if it's a mixed age team. My daughter's town team is comprised of 7th graders and 8th graders and you can see the girls stand in groups by age.

As a coach, one easy way to get girls to connect with players other than the ones they tend towards naturally is to form groups by counting off. This naturally splits up cliques.

I like to find ways to connect girls through forming groups. Some ideas are:

- By age: make a line from youngest to oldest. The coach can then partition off groups.
- By pets: if you have a cat, you're to my right. If you have a dog, you're to my left. Girls without pets or have other pets, in front of me.

- By extracurricular activity: if you play an instrument, to my right. If you've ever performed in a play or sang a solo, to my left. Everyone else in front of me.

- By books: if you read a book for pleasure today, to my right. If you plan to read a book for pleasure today, on my left. If you are not reading today, in front of me.

- By school subject: if your favorite class is Math, to my left. If it's English, over here. If it's Science, you're a group. History lovers over here.

- Not in a carpool: from a group with someone you've never carpooled with.

- Not on a team together previously: form a group with girls you've never played with previously.

It's really important to break up groups, not just because of cliques, but because it's very intimidating for girls to form a group with players who they think are more skilled than they are. They are never naturally going to do this. It's down to a confidence issue.

It's amazing how fast a new group will form a bond and be laughing together. When girls are put into a group where they don't have a social connection, they find ways to connect with each other. These bonds make for a stronger team and can last off the field, and even continue when they no longer play together. It's amazing how such a small thing – forcing girls into groups that they would not voluntarily form – can change the dynamic of a team in such a positive way.

I recommend forming new groups as a routine part of every practice. It will strengthen existing bonds and form new ones.

SUMMARY

- Girls naturally form groups based on who they socially know.

- It's up to the coach to break up cliques by setting the rules to form groups during practice.

- One easy way to form groups is to count off which naturally breaks up cliques.

- Other ideas for forming groups can help the players find connections with girls that they don't know.

- It's important to constantly create different groups during practices, as this creates team bonding and helps weaker players to find connections with stronger players.

I try to mix up the team to get them to interact with each other. Early in the season, everyone goes into their friend groups but later in the year, I try to mix it up to get veterans with newbies, in order to get everyone talking to each other. With nearly sixty team members and just one coach, it's a challenge to manage. Some of my team are ready to ski in college, while nearly half of the team is new to the sport. Getting veterans to share their experience with newbies makes for a better team. One of the things with having such a big team with mixed boys and girls, is that you have to teach everyone the same things but they learn at different speeds. I use the resources that I have, and have seniors with knowledge help teach the younger, new skiers. Mixing up the team to get them out of their usual high school social groups is a key to coaching such a large team but it also makes for better team cohesiveness.

Chandra Wisneski – Girls and Boys Nordic Ski Coach for Freshman, JV and Varsity teams, Newton North High School, Massachusetts

13 | The Pitfalls of Choosing Captains

Mia: *My daughter was on a new club soccer team in which half the team were friends of hers from a previous team. The captain selection process seemed arbitrary. Right before every game, the coach would need a captain to start the game, and she tended to choose the same person, Anna*. Anna is a good player – although there's at least a half dozen players at her level – and she's a good friend of my daughter's, as they had played on the same team the previous year. Even though the captain's duties on this team were solely to represent the team before the game started and determine who kicked-off, my daughter felt like Anna was the 'coach's pet' and resented her and the coach.*

Alison: Girls are not developmentally ready to have permanent captains for a sports season or an academic year until they are at least 18 years old. It doesn't matter whether these captains are assigned by the coach or chosen by the team members themselves through a voting process.

> Peer leadership is very difficult. Having an assigned captain or captains gives power to one person too early on, which makes for poor followers.

Ask yourself, who usually gets chosen as a captain on a sports team? The answer is generally the strongest and most skilled player. This athlete already has status by way of her skills, and in fact, the most skilled athlete may not actually feel comfortable leading the team. She may not have the personality or abilities to lead at this moment in time. Additional recognition of one person can lead to feelings of isolation amongst their peers, which in turn can make the captain wary of leading. It might not necessarily be the best experience for her to be thrust into a leadership position if the rest of the team isn't on board.

Team members who don't get a chance to lead and find this frustrating may undermine the captain both with words and actions. A sense of team can quickly deteriorate. There is an easy solution to the situation; giving the responsibility of the captainship to everyone teaches the importance of being a gracious follower and creates better leaders.

Create positive leaders and followers

Teaching how to follow is as important as teaching how to lead.

My recommendation would be to **rotate all the players on a team into a leadership position** at least once a season. Players are developmentally ready to take on the role of captain starting at age nine.

The easiest way to assign captains is for a set period of time, such as two weeks. If you have too many players and not enough weeks in a season, have multiple co-captains.

Use the role of captain as a learning opportunity for the team at the beginning of the season. Here are some examples of responsibilities that can be assigned to the captain:

- Make sure teammates are on time.
- Ensure everyone is ready for warm up.
- When the coach is talking, ask everyone to pay attention.
- Lead the team warm-up to begin practice and before a game.

- Jog players in for a coach huddle or coach instructions.
- Set up equipment for drills during practice.
- Clean up equipment on the field after the game.
- Give motivational/inspirational pump-ups before games.
- Meet with the referee at the beginning of each game for the coin toss to determine which team kicks off.

The beauty of a rotating captain schedule is that every athlete gets a turn, and realizes that when it's her turn, if she's a good follower for a captain, she can expect the same in return. This also gives every athlete the chance to find their voice and character in a way that makes their peers want to follow.

In this way, captains realize the value of having good followers. Getting teammates to be good followers can be earned by doing the same for them; every athlete realizes that when it's her turn, she will want her teammates to be good followers, and the process turns into a collaborative effort … and that's the definition of a good team.

One way to celebrate this team unity is for the coach to pass an arm band from one captain to the next each week. If there are co-captains each week, the arm band can be split during the game. When it's the player(s) turn for the week, they write their initials on the inside of the arm band. At the end of the season, the arm band becomes a symbol of collective leadership. The coach could gift the arm band at the end of the year celebration to the best follower, for example, and who helped make every player a successful captain.

Rotating the role of captain teaches everyone the importance of being a good teammate

SUMMARY

- Having the same captain or captains for a season or year is not age appropriate for girls until they are at least 18 years old.

- Create positive leaders and followers.

- Rotating the role of captain ensures each athlete gets a turn. This is age appropriate starting at U9.

- Set up a schedule for the role of captain at the beginning of each season, and clearly state the responsibilities of the position. Increase the responsibilities for older girls in an age appropriate way.

- Being a captain will teach the value of being a good follower.

- Buy a captain armband that rotates each week. Ask each captain to write her initials on the inside of the band when it's her week. It's a symbol of collective leadership that can be awarded at the end of the season.

- Teach female athletes how to be a good teammate. This means being a good follower as well as a good leader, which in turn becomes a collaborative system.

One of my favorite team building exercises is our selection process for captains. As a team, we sit down and go through the characteristics of what makes a good leader, as well as those that don't make a good leader. Each player has their own mindset of what they look for in a leader and I ask everyone to verbalize their opinions in a group setting. It's very informal and all thoughts are written on a white board for everyone to see. It's an opportunity for the entire team to hear what each individual feels, and can lead to an understanding of why a captain was voted for. I think of it as a team building experience because we don't often talk about leadership with the team, but most players leave the meeting with new ideas from her teammates on what it takes to lead a group.

Kelly Doton, Boston College, Head Coach Women's Field Hockey

14 | Handling a Losing Streak

Mia: *Let's face it: winning feels pretty good. That being said, it's the coach who determines the team's focus. When my oldest started playing club volleyball, her team lost every game the entire season. What was amazing though, was how her coaches made her feel; because the focus was on development, their coach made them feel like winners because he could see visible improvement from game to game. He told them how proud he was of them and noted specific instances of how the team had improved. It turns out, it's not whether you win or lose, but how the team performs based on the goals the coach sets for the team. Setting goals around team chemistry and development for the players is a more powerful message, both for sport and in life. The coach has the ability to transcend the focus from winning to something bigger and more inclusive.*

Alison: The first place to begin when creating team culture as a coach is to define the team goals. What do we want to get out of our season? For me, team goals do not include a win/loss record. Instead, they are focused on team chemistry. I believe that the wins will come automatically if there is good team work in the form of solid team chemistry.

Typically, a volunteer parent coach isn't being evaluated on their win/loss record. So, if the team record isn't being used to evaluate us as coaches, what are the other measurements that we are considering? Usually the priorities of the volunteer coaches are based on whether they are creating a healthy environment, and emanating positivity. My goal was to ensure that all the kids wanted to continue playing because it was fun!

Here's an example of a goal based on excellent team comradery. We want to make sure that our team chemistry is exceptional; because we have some new players on our team this year, one target is to ask each player to get to know two or three players who they didn't know beforehand. This goal supports our focus on having fun, and on developing excellent teamwork/team chemistry.

We may set the team goals for our season as these:

- Having fun
- Player development
- Team development
- Respect
- Team chemistry/teamwork

It's also important to note that winning is not necessarily a measure of individual or team development. Progress doesn't always transform into winning. We need to teach this at a young age: we might be getting better, but we might not always win.

> Progress doesn't always transform into winning. We might be getting better, but we might not always win. This is an important message to teach at a young age.

Besides our goal of superb team chemistry, we might also have one or two team development goals that we are working on during practices and games. After a game, it's important to go back to these development goals and talk about the team's progress towards them. Here's an example of a post-game wrap up meeting:

"One of the goals we set this week was to move the ball out of the back. We moved the ball so much better out of the back today. We

asked the team to not just kick the ball forward but to get it to a teammate's feet, and I was really proud of the team for doing that today."

It's also appropriate to compliment the opponent. For example, if an opponent is skilled at taking corners, that would be verbalized, and we would identify that one of our team goals for the following week is to work on defending against corners.

> *You could be really good, but that doesn't mean you always win.*

I would also end each meeting with some positive feedback. It could be as a team, or it could be about an individual. It could be that we tried to improve on a harder skill.

Losing should also be viewed as something that is a positive learning tool. It makes us evaluate how we are doing a little more closely. It helps us identify specific things to work on. There's 'winning ugly', but it doesn't necessarily make the players better. The value of losing and using this to improve is a valuable lesson that we can teach our players, and one that they can use throughout their lives.

During a losing streak, you still have to find things to celebrate. You need to find things to keep kids motivated. I'd base it on the progress the team is making. The post-game wrap up becomes critical. Win or lose, you want to identify two or three things that the team did well that you had been working on in training. The message is that the hard work that everyone is putting in is resulting in improvement, and that the wins will come.

It's difficult when there is a losing streak because parents complain, but always reference back to that first parent meeting when the team goals were communicated: having fun, individual development, team development, respect, and team chemistry.

If you measure me as the volunteer coach based on wins and losses, you are on the wrong team.

You can also communicate to parents that if they want to measure you as a coach based on wins and losses, they are on the wrong team. We are going to evaluate ourselves on other criteria.

It's essential that the coach remains steady. Win or lose, the team needs to keep its usual rituals post-game, whether it's a team cool down jog and stretch or a team cheer. The coach has to be the same person, no matter what the outcome of the game. The positive message the coach communicates during the post-game wrap up will send the players off on a high note. You might also want to consider building in a post-game ritual of a fun activity, whether it's a team snack or a celebration of a player's birthday, or a team cheer.

SUMMARY

- In the initial team meeting with parents and players, state your goals for the team this season and note that it does NOT include a win/loss percentage.

- Team chemistry, having fun, individual and team development are great team goals.

- In addition to these general goals, have two to three specific development goals for the team each week.

- Focus post-game wrap up meetings based on those two to three specific team development goals and give positive feedback on improvement towards those goals.

- Use losing as a learning tool to identify team skills to work on during practice next week.

- Remain steady as a coach, whether the team wins or loses, and continue with the same post-game rituals, including at least one fun one.

- Find things to celebrate, either individual or with reference to team skill development.

- Go back to the fun factor; is the team having fun?

- Communicate to players that losing is a learning opportunity to identify where to improve. This is a great life lesson about working hard towards long term goals and not being afraid to fail.

- It's usually the parents who care about the win/loss record, not the kids.

15 | Supporting multi-sport athletes

Mia: *My daughter had only participated in team sports such as soccer and rowing when she decided to try out a new sport, Nordic Skiing (cross country skiing) in order to represent her high school. In this sport, she was the 'newbie' who was far from the best. But she and her friends, though novices, brought an infectious team spirit by cheering loudly at races and awards banquets where support was typically more muted.*

They made a lot of friends by simply inquiring about how other athlete's races went, and providing emotional support when their new friends were unhappy with their results. It turns out that no one had really done that in the past. In return, she appreciated the simplicity of performance evaluation. Ranking based solely on her time was a break from a more subjective evaluation. My daughter still views Nordic Skiing as her 'off-season' sport, but the benefits were both emotionally and physically positive.

Alison: The statistic that 70% of kids leave organized sports before middle school is a staggering one. As a coach, we can affect this number if we focus on getting our players to return to sports each season. One significant way is to offer support and flexibility when they are willing to play more than one sport in a season, or want to try out a different sport during the off-season.

70% of kids quit organized sports before middle school.

The trend to specialize in one sport is a major contributor to athletes leaving sport altogether before the age of 13. A single sport athlete tends to feel more pressure to perform and suffers more risk of injury from repetitive motion. As a coach, we can provide immense encouragement to multi-sport athletes by simply providing permission to let them decide how to juggle conflicting demands. At the end of the day, if the athlete misses practices or games for one sport, she is probably getting a similar workout from her other sport.

> *Less than 7% percent of high school athletes move on to college sports.**

*From NCAA 2017 Probability of Competing Beyond High School Figures and Methodology.

With less than 7% percent of high school athletes moving on to college sports, allowing our players to participate in multiple sports gives them a greater opportunity to play in organized sports as adults.

Playing different sports prevents burnout.

Training in a variety of sports prevents burnout and injury. Most athletes who play different sports will have different levels of aptitude for each sport. Playing their 'fun' sport gives them a mental break. Some athletes change up their sports to maintain a high level of fitness because their main sport may have a down period. Utilizing different muscle groups helps with injury prevention and is especially important for sports with repetitive motion, such as cross country running. Training in different sports with drills and practices that feel new make training fun.

By giving athletes the space to try new sports, we are reinforcing our primary message that this is for fun.

Cross training for crossover skills.

Different sports utilize different skills and work different muscle groups. Skills from one sport crossover in subtle and powerful ways. Developing skills like hand-eye coordination, endurance, balance, agility, explosive power, focus and concentration, fast decision making, or leadership crosses over from one sport to another. For example, tap dancing can help soccer athletes with better foot control. Boxing develops faster reflexes useful for almost any sport. Yoga teaches athletes mindfulness and can bring a sense of calm during a time of stress. This is incredibly useful in any high-pressure situation, including competitions and games.

Multi-team athletes are better teammates.

Socially, participating in different sports enable girls to meet a wider variety and greater number of people. Perhaps one team is based more on where they go to school. Another team may have more socio-economic and ethnic diversity than that school team. Other teams may have a wider range of geographic distribution, allowing girls to get a glimpse of other areas that might be new to them.

Athletes who play team sports as well as individual sports also get exposed to different ways of evaluation and measurement, making them more resilient. Individual sports with a clear measurement for winning such as tennis or track and field provide data based feedback in terms of points and times. Team sports that rely on a group performance have different criteria for evaluation that can be more subjective.

Trying new sports also gives girls the opportunity to be the 'new' player; the outsider who isn't skilled in the sport. Girls get to feel what it's like not to be the best athlete on the team. This in turn can make them become more empathetic when they return to their 'main' sport. It supports Growth Mindset by showing them that while their natural ability may vary from sport to sport, working hard is the key to mastering skills.

Multi-sport athletes learn to compete in a wide variety of ways.

Different sports can feel very different during competition and encourage participants to learn to compete in varying conditions, requiring a wide range of skill sets that can cross over to other sports, as well as life.

Athletes who play repetitive motion sports need to get into a more relaxed meditative mental state when competing, such as distance swimmer and runners, as opposed to athletes who make quick, frequent decisions such as boxers and soccer players.

Weather conditions also add variety. Athletes who play indoor sports, such as volleyball, can learn a lot about adaption when playing an outdoor sport such as rugby that competes in a range of weather conditions from freezing rain to steamy humidity.

Some sports require long periods of intense concentration such as softball, and encourage participants to master focus and patience. Contrast that to the short periods of high focus intensity required in fencing.

Sports also requires different levels of communication amongst teammates. Team sports such as volleyball and soccer require constant communication to execute plays. Individual sports don't need the same level of communication during competitions, but a different style of communication to create a sense of team.

The different requirements of each sport allow athletes to develop a whole range of skills that are applicable to life.

Sports for Life Skills. Sports for Life.

Certain sports are harder to participate in as adults whether because of the challenge of forming a team or finding a facility to train at or because they require a fitness level that is hard to maintain as adults. Letting kids participate in a range of sports encourages them to find something that will last a lifetime and that will maintain their fitness through to their adult lives.

From a Growth Mindset point of view, allowing children to try different sports reinforces the message that proficiency is the result of effort. The players who are willing to take the risk of trying something new will benefit from knowing that while they won't be the best athlete when they start, it's a rewarding experience worth pursuing.

SUMMARY

- 70% of kids quit organized sports before middle school.
- Less than 7% percent of high school athletes move on to college sports.
- Letting athletes participate in multiple sports allows them the chance to play sports for life.
- Specialization in sports increases the chance of injury.
- Multi-sport athletes can make better teammates.
- Multi-sport athletes learn to compete in a wide range of situations.
- Both physical and mental skills transfers from one sport to the next, and can also transfer to skills we need in everyday life.

16 Body Image, Puberty and Sports

Mia: *Navigating body image as girls go through puberty is challenging. Add in sports and there is a further level of complexity. On the one hand, sport teaches girls that their bodies are to be celebrated for what they are: strong and capable. On the other hand, media informs girls that they are being evaluated solely on their appearance. As a parent, this drama plays out in small ways: is there an after-game team snack and does it have to be 'healthy'?*

I was that mom. My middle daughter who played a lot of soccer was usually the smallest girl on the field. A match-up with a girl much taller seemed like a doomed proposition. Team snacks were also a minefield that had to be carefully considered for parental approval, and I usually provided multiple options just to be safe. However, this was just the tip of the iceberg.

My oldest daughter played on a town soccer team with a volunteer dad coach who also happened to teach at one of our local middle schools. My daughter was in an awkward phase of puberty; she would gain weight first and stay the same height for a long time, before shooting up. She also had knee problems caused by tight hamstrings and puberty and often couldn't participate because of the pain. Her coach was unsympathetic, and called her out in front of her teammates for being lazy and unfit. This ended up being the last year she played soccer.

Alison: Even a decade ago, I noticed that young girls in the age range of 11 and 12 weren't focusing on their bodies. But now puberty is happening at a younger age. There's also a trend for more form-fitting soccer uniforms; even the kits for U12 girls are designed to be slimmer which can make girls more conscious of their bodies. One consequence of these trends is that some young girls will restrict their eating, and that's where the coach can come in and be a positive influence.

> We, as coaches, have to be careful how we describe girls' bodies: "Girls in the back are BIG." Nobody wants to be that 'big' girl.

Don't Talk About Size

The language used by coaches to describe girls' bodies is very powerful and something that girls really take to heart. It can be as simple as splitting a team into two groups: big girls versus small girls. That's a very forceful negative reinforcement to those larger girls. It might seem simple, but those words can be damaging.

Puberty complicates the issue of body image because girls' bodies are changing so rapidly. However, the stigma of labeling any girl by size can lead to devastating consequences, including food restriction with carbohydrate avoidance; girls going through puberty *need* carbohydrates. A coach can be a positive influence by always remaining conscious of how he or she makes reference to girls' bodies.

I never describe my team by size. To me, it's not about size. We have all shapes and sizes. But hearing a team described by their size is actually very common. Take, for example, the Notre Dame team who have many tall players. I've heard people say: "All the girls are massive at Notre Dame." I have even heard this description regarding a town team: "We don't know what's in the water, but they are massive down there." No girl wants to be described as "massive." When you use that terminology, the girls hear: "What

I'm putting inside of me is making me massive."

Coaches should never describe girls by size in any context. For example: "The defenders in the back are BIG." A 'big' girl could, in reality, be tall, lean and underweight, but in her head, she may hear 'big as 'overweight'. There are also girls who feel uncomfortable in tight uniforms and are particularly sensitive to language connoting size. You might notice them tugging on their uniform, trying to pull it down.

The description of 'Big versus Small' has negative connotations to all players. It is not empowering for a girl to hear the message that she is 'small'. Girls who haven't gone through puberty may be smaller in size, but I don't want them to feel timid or weak compared to girls who have developed faster. If they feel that their size is an issue, it is important for the coach to turn it into a positive. Instead of size, use skill to reinforce a positive message:

- Speed and quickness for a 'small' player: This is a great match-up for you because you are so fast you can spin them around.

- Powerful Weapon for a 'big' player: You have a powerful weapon of long ball distribution.

Food has to be thought of as positive without overanalyzing it

One alarming trend of girls hitting puberty at a younger age is that some girls restrict their food. They may think this will make them fitter or faster. They may believe that they need to take healthy eating to an extreme in order to be a competitive player. If they are in an awkward phase of puberty, they may think being thinner will make them look better in that tight uniform.

We need to talk positively about nutrition. It's fuel for our bodies. It makes us faster. We need carbohydrates for energy. Food = Energy

I really believe the most important message that coaches can give female players is the power of food for performance. Food is fuel that allows you to perform, it is a means to your success. Fill up that tank for production! Everything in moderation! During games, my college players on the bench are given chocolate, peanut butter, and granola. Players who are in middle school and younger who come to my soccer camps can buy candy from our Tuck Shop. It's part of what makes camp fun.

Not all coaches are happy with encouraging cake and candy for kids playing sports. Some coaches at U12 are breaking down information on amounts of protein, and recommending recovery drink post-games. Kids at U12 don't need recovery drinks. It's confusing for them to get too much information about what to eat. It also sends a message that places the emphasis on winning and 'professionalism', which is not age appropriate and which is the opposite of the one we want them to receive about playing sport for fun.

I think a coaches' message for game preparation should be simple. Eat a healthy meal. Eat from the four food groups. In fact, I would emphasize telling players to get a good night's sleep and staying hydrated over what to eat or drink.

As for what is healthy versus unhealthy for a game or post-game snack, the snack conveys a message to girls that they hear loud and clear. Coaches are going in a direction at the youth platform of conveying that nutrition will give kids a competitive edge. An emphasis on a snack for nutritional value conveys a message of the important of performance and winning.

However, a post-game snack can also convey that we play this sport because it's fun. Why not celebrate after a game with cake? It's more constructive to send a positive message around food, not a restrictive one.

Pre-Game Preparation: Emphasize eating a healthy meal with carbohydrates to fuel you. Get a good night's sleep. Stay hydrated.

Half-Time Snack: A snack at half time is not a necessity, but can be replenishing. Orange slices to help stay hydrated and fueled sends a good message.

Post-Game Snack: Post-game for young girls this age should not be about replenishing the body, but more about a celebration to emphasize the message that this team experience is about having fun. We just had a game – win, lose or draw – let's celebrate! It's okay to have cake. A post-game snack does NOT have to be healthy (and technically, post-game is the best time to have fat in your system).

Do sports drinks enhance performance?

There is no scientific evidence that sports drinks enhance performance. We have to be very careful about presenting nutritional advice at too young an age to girls. But you can use sports drinks as a reward or celebration, just like letting them have cake or candy as a post-game snack.

The coach has the ability to make a positive impact on how girls feel about their bodies and about their performance. The connection of these two things can go a very long way into influencing their personal relationships and their self-worth.

SUMMARY

- Be careful about the language you use as a coach to describe girls' bodies.

- Avoid referring to girls by size.

- Food should be thought of as positive without giving too much instruction on how to eat.

- Keep the instructions the night before games simple: a healthy meal with carbohydrates, a good night's sleep, stay hydrated.

- Post-game snack is not about replenishing so does not have to be 'healthy'.

SOLUTIONS TO
SPECIFIC ISSUES – *NOTES*

PRE-SEASON
PLANNING

· ·

PRE-SEASON PLANNING

17 | Player Code of Conduct

Mia: *My daughters rarely received a formal Player Code of Conduct that they had to read and sign for the sports teams that they played on. I like a formal players' contract to put everyone on the same page at the start of a new season. Without a formal list of rules, the players have to deduce what the coach's rules of conduct are, and the unspoken rules of behavior can take longer to figure out (e.g. are we here to win or have fun?).*

Champions make those around them better.

Alison: At the start of the season, go over the Player Code of Conduct and then ask each player to sign as a statement that they understand and commit to this. This is a great opportunity to set the tone of the team: teamwork, having fun, mutual respect.

- Have fun!
- Show courtesy and respect to all coaches, players, opponents, officials, parents, and fans.
- Attend every practice and game that you can, and notify the coach if you can't make it.
- Be supportive of teammates.
- Winning isn't everything. We are here to have fun, play fairly, improve our skills, and make friends.

- Learn the rules and play by them.
- Talk to the coach directly about any issues or concerns.

This Champion's Creed is a popular accompaniment to the Player's Code of Conduct. I like to keep the Player's Code of Conduct simple and concise so the kids can focus on the big picture message. The Champion's Creed gives inspirational examples of good sportsmanship and helps shape players into good people.

> *Champions know winning is not necessarily measured by the final score.*

The Champion's Creed

Champions get up one more time than they have been knocked down

Champions give their all, no matter the score

Champions do what is right, even when it hurts

Champions know winning is not necessarily measured by the final score

Champions take a stand for what is right, even when they stand alone

Champions see every challenge as an opportunity

Champions make those around them better

Champions do the right thing, even when no one is watching

Champions dedicate themselves to prepare for success

Champions put the success of others above individual achievement

Champions understand winning is not the only thing

Champions live by a higher personal standard

Champions stand firm when others around them fall

Champions live by what they speak and speak what they live

Champions lay down their own desires for the benefit of others

Champions willingly accept responsibility, and graciously deflect honor

Champions never sacrifice what is best for something good

Champions may fail … but they never quit

SUMMARY

- A players' contract helps get everyone on the same page regarding team culture.

- Go over the players' contract at the start of the season and ask every player to sign the contract. This is a good time to emphasize the coach's primary goals: having fun, development, and good sportsmanship.

- The players' contract encourages self-advocacy by having them go directly to the coach for issues or concerns.

- The Champion's Creed further illustrates good sportsmanship with specific examples as well as applying Growth Mindset to sports.

18 | Parent Code of Conduct

Mia: *70% of kids drop out of organized sports by age 13. As parents, what we say during the game and especially on the ride home heavily influences how our kids feel about their experience. Are we focusing on having fun versus winning? Are we coaching from the sidelines when we are not actually the coach? Do our kids feel like mistakes are learning opportunities?*

I think we've all been on the sidelines and witnessed parents yelling at referees, their child, the opposition's coach, or even their child's own coach. The only way to curb bad behavior is to have the coach set clear expectations with a Parent Code of Conduct agreement. But how do we enforce this code of conduct? My daughter's soccer coach would call a mandatory meeting for all parents after a practice every time there was an infraction. This was extremely inconvenient for the parents of children in carpools. After one such meeting, parents would remind other parents on the team of the rules during games because no one wanted to stay late to attend more meetings about the Parent Code of Conduct.

Parent Code of Conduct

Alison: Setting clear parent expectations at the start of the season goes a long way into creating a positive team atmosphere. As part of your Team Orientation Packet, include a Parent/Athlete Code of Conduct and have both the parents and athlete sign an agreement. This is an opportunity to set clear expectations and goals for the team, both athletes and parents. You might want to start with overall goals such as:

- Having fun

- 100% of kids on the team signing again next season
- Developmentally appropriate skills and tactics

I think it's important for parents to know that by age 14, girls drop out of sports at twice the rate of boys*, and thus the goal of having fun and continued participation are actually quite ambitious goals. But how do kids define 'fun' with regard to sports?

*Girls drop-out at different rates depending on where they live. Sabo, D. and Veliz, P. (2008). Go Out and Play: Youth Sports in America. East Meadow, NY: Women's Sports Foundation.

> 9 of 10 kids said 'fun' is the main reason they play sports. Out of the 81 reasons kids said sports were fun, 'winning' ranked as 48. Young girls gave 'winning' the lowest ratings.*

*Amanda J. Visek, Sara M. Achrati, Heather Manning, Karen McDonnell, Brandonn S. Harris, and Loretta DiPietro. The Fun Integration Theory: Towards Sustaining Children and Adolescents Sport Participation. Journal of Physical Activity and Health. 2015 Mar; 12(3): 424–433.

In the Fun Integration Theory study referenced below, the top six things that children found the most fun in sports were:

1. Trying your best.
2. When the coach treats the player with respect.
3. Getting playing time.
4. Playing well together as a team.
5. Getting along with your teammates.
6. Exercising and being active.

Winning ranked 48th out of 81 factors defining fun in sports by kids. In young girls, winning ranked even lower. It's clear that having fun is not related to winning in the eyes of these athletes. Parents need to understand that pressure to perform creates a negative environment and is a high contribution factor towards kids leaving sports before they reach high school.

That's where a Parent Code of Conduct is crucial; it can set expectations and educate parents on what's important to you, as the coach.

Parent Code of Conduct

This Parent/Athlete Code of Conduct is short but specific, and works for all sports. It's from the New England U16 Nordic Ski Championships.

Make New Friends and Have Fun

This Massachusetts team is comprised of skiers from all over the state. This is an opportunity to get to know new people and make new friends as we work together to ski our hardest, do our best, and have a lot of fun. (*This can be modified for any sport or team.*)

Exemplify Good Sportsmanship

Competition can present emotions from disappointment to elation. Focus on what you can control and the positives of the competitive experience, rather than wallowing in despair after an unsatisfying result.

Parents: Set a Good Example

Give your child unconditional love and support. Let the coaches provide constructive feedback and technical support to the athletes. Do not coach or instruct your child from the sidelines.

Parents of athletes are asked to set an example for our children by being respectful of all coaches' and officials' decisions, staying positive and supportive, and encouraging all the athletes. Parents, too, are asked to be 'team players' by looking at what's best for the whole team rather than individual athletes.

- Bring a positive and supportive attitude.
- Respect all participants, coaches, parents, and officials.
- Good sportsmanship and encouragement of others is expected at all times.
- Be the ultimate team player. Consider others before yourself and do what's right for the team.
- Do not coach from the sidelines.
- Do not engage in game-related discussions with parents from the opposing team.
- Never address players from the opposing team except to encourage.
- Leave the game on the field.

Here's specific advice on what parents can and should say before and after games.

Before the game:

1. I love you
2. Have fun
3. Good luck

After the game:

1. I love you
2. I really enjoyed watching you play
3. Did you have fun?

SUMMARY

- 70% of kids stop playing sports before high school because it's no longer fun.
- Kids do not define 'fun' in sports with winning. In fact, young girls rank winning as one of the lowest factors for having fun in sports.
- Distribute a written Parent Code of Conduct before the season begins.
- Go over the Parent Code of Conduct during the team orientation meeting, if you have one.
- Have parents sign the Parent Code of Conduct.
- Hold a mandatory parent meeting every time there is an infraction of Parent Code of Conduct during a game.

19 | Creating Your Medical Emergency Plan

Mia: *My kids get nosebleeds. We refer to them as 'gushers'. For the uninitiated, it looks like they are bleeding out at a frightening rate. The real issue, though, is keeping the blood off their uniforms, because they can't go back into play during a game with blood stained clothes, and they definitely want to keep playing once their nosebleed has ended. My kids know what to do when the nosebleed ensues, but invariably no one has tissues, and sometimes my car is parked quite a distance away. Even if I jog to my car, they are literally holding the blood in their cupped hands, trying to keep it off their clothes. Finally, I made them each a "nose bleed kit" for their sports backpacks. I include four packs of travel tissue packs, one pack of baby wipes, Band-Aids, and an ice pack. It usually gets used at least once per season, either for themselves or to help out a teammate.*

Alison: Concussions are at the front of every coach's mind. If an athlete hits her head, that's it, you can't allow her to come back in.

What if the wind is knocked out of her? This is when an assistant coach or an assigned rotating parent helper provides another set of hands during a game or practice. I have that person sit with the player while you call 911.

What's your emergency plan? It's a good idea to create this before the season begins and I recommend the following:

- A Medical Release form, filled in by the parents, listing any allergies and existing medical conditions
- Cell phone numbers of all the parents, making sure you have the numbers for both parents

- If you don't have an assistant coach, set up a parent rotation for the games at least, to ensure that there is someone to sit with the players and help-out

- A well-stocked medical kit to take to practices and games

- A medical procedure plan that is part of the email communication of expectations to parents

Medical Procedure Plan

For each type of injury, what is the plan?

Head Injury/Concussion: player sits out. No exceptions.

Possible Fracture: player comes off the field after an injury, and the coach talks to the parent/s to get their permission as to whether the player should return to the game. You'll need the parents' cell phone number if the player carpooled, and doesn't have a parent on the sidelines. You want a clear plan of who makes the call if the player goes back in. A fracture isn't always obvious until after the game from an X-Ray and the coach doesn't necessarily want to make the decision as to whether or not the player should return to the game because of liability issues.

Nosebleed: Player comes off the field until bleeding stops. If a uniform becomes bloodstained, a player cannot return to the field, so an extra kit is useful.

Emergency Medical Kit for Practices and Games

- Roll of toilet paper or large box of tissues (also comes in handy for those locations where there are no bathroom facilities).

- Cotton wool soaked in Otrivin for nose bleeds.

- Baby wipes.

- Ice packs.

- Band-Aids.

- Cell phone numbers of all the parents.

- Latex Gloves.

- Saline and contact cases for players with contacts.

- A back-up pair of contacts for all players who wear contacts in case they lose one. Ask each player to put their contact lenses in a labeled zip lock bag.

- Plastic bags to dispose of bloody gauze, etc.

- Hydrogen Peroxide (very useful for getting blood out of a jersey).

- Feminine hygiene products for teenage girls.

- REMEMBER: Put your emergency medical kit in the car and bring it out during practices and games, just as you would with other equipment such as cones and balls.

SUMMARY

- Keep the team's medical release forms with information on allergies and pre-existing medical conditions with you at *all times*.

- Have an assigned adult helping you at games and practices. They can be an assistant coach or a rotation of parents.

- Keep a list handy of all the parents' cell phone numbers.

- Get explicit permission from parents if their child should return to the game after a field injury.

- In the case of head injury, the player does NOT return to the game.

- Make an Emergency Medical Kit and bring it on the field to all the practices and games.

20 Player Goals and Evaluations

Mia: *Not all coaches give player evaluations I've noticed. My middle daughter received formal player evaluations when she played soccer, starting from the time she was in middle school. Both her town team coach and her club team coach gave written reviews, but with different frequencies. Her town team coach gave weekly performance evaluations after every game. Not all her teammates liked getting graded weekly, but I thought it was great. Her club team coach gave written evaluations twice a year at the end of each season, but also did a face-to-face meeting to go over the form. I've saved all these forms and it's fun to look back on them to see what she was working on, and her progress that year. In any format (written or verbal), feedback is crucial for player development. The delivery of the feedback is critical though. Even though my daughter got mostly positive feedback, she worried about her face-to-face assessment. After each evaluation meeting though, she would have a giant smile on her face!*

Alison: For volunteer parent coaches, the first thing to consider when thinking about individual player goals and evaluations is how much time you have to dedicate to it, and therefore the frequency that you can realistically commit to. It's not necessary as a parent volunteer coach to do formal written evaluations. The important thing is to have players feel good about themselves.

Positive verbal feedback versus written evaluation.

It's time consuming, but girls need feedback. Constant positive verbal feedback during practices is sufficient for girls younger than middle school, but if you have the time, a face-to-face evaluation at the end of each season can be a powerful way of letting each player know how much you appreciate their efforts. You can also use this time to help them set development goals for next season.

It's not necessary as a parent volunteer coach to do formal written evaluations. The important thing is to have players feel good about themselves.

Age appropriateness of player evaluations.

There's a few factors to consider when deciding if you want to do written player evaluations:

- Age of player.
- If you feel comfortable giving this type of feedback given your experience and level of knowledge as a coach.
- Your time availability.
- Level of the player's commitment to improve.

I think that written evaluations can be synched up to letter grades at school. That is to say, at some point in middle school most children start to get their first academic letter grades. This is also when I would recommend a formal written and face-to-face evaluation process.

There's also your time availability to consider. As a parent volunteer coach, additional time to create player evaluations might not be feasible. Verbal feedback during practices is where the real learning and impact is. A written evaluation is really the summary of all the verbal feedback you have already given in practices. If you don't have time for a formal evaluation process, it's not a problem.

Finally, you need to consider how much your players are seeking evaluations. You can gauge this by their time commitment. Did your team consistently show up for all practices? Were they serious about wanting to practice and improve, or was it hard to get them to focus as opposed to socializing? If your sense is that this particular sporting experience wasn't the priority for the majority of your team and that they won't be focusing on it in the upcoming years, then it's fine to concentrate on having fun and less on written evaluations.

Once you have decided that written evaluations make sense, using a form helps to organize and standardize your feedback. Here are some examples of player evaluations that can work across all sports. There's also a skill section that is specific to soccer, but which can be switched for another sport's technical skills.

This is a five-point grading scale: 5 Excellent, 4 Very Good, 3 Good, 2 Needs Improvement.

Each skill is rated 2-5 with a short comment.

☐ Works Hard in Practice

☐ Leads by Example

☐ Sportsmanship

☐ Team Player

☐ Agility

☐ Quickness

☐ Aggression

☐ Endurance

☐ Overall Fitness

☐ Dribbling

☐ Ball control

☐ Passing

☐ Shooting

☐ Field Awareness

☐ Position Awareness

Summary Comments:

....

....

....

....

....

....

....

....

....

....

....

Here's another example of a player evaluation for soccer.

General Comments:

☐ Dribbling and Ball Control:

☐ Passing and Serving:

☐ Receiving and First Touch:

☐ Shooting, Crossing, Striking:

☐ Speed (i.e. first to the ball):

☐ Fitness:

☐ Defensive Techniques:

☐ Game Sense:

☐ Positioning, Spacing on the Field:

☐ Focus during the Game:

Things to Work on in the Upcoming Weeks:

....

....

....

....

....

....

....

Give every player a certificate with award categories that recognize good sportsmanship in addition to ability.

Another entertaining way to end the season in terms of feedback is to recognize the skills of every player at the end of the season. This can be done with a certificate presentation, and with a little story about each player. It can be carried out informally after the last game during the post-game meeting. One coach even gave out these awards accompanied by a candy bar that best represented that player's quality (i.e. Most Positive got an Almond Joy).

Most Positive

Best Free Kick

Best Assist

Best Goal

Best Penalty Kick

Best Throw In

Best Save

Best Passer

Best Attitude

Hardest Working

Most Dedicated

Beast Award for Defending

Best Cheerleader

Most Responsible

Most Inclusive

Most Motivating

Fashionista

Never Gives Up

Coolest Cleats

Fastest Runner/Highest Jumper (volleyball)

Most Passionate

Most Improved

Most Knowledgeable About the Sport

Last One Off the Field

Always Willing to Help Out

Most Supportive

Most Focused

Performance Under Pressure

Risk Taker

Not Afraid to Try

Fun Award

Clutch Award

SUMMARY

- Give frequent positive verbal feedback during practices and games.

- Written player evaluations are helpful at the end of each season, but not necessary.

- Before committing to written evaluations, consider your time availability, the age of the players and their level of commitment.

- Awards to every player at the end of the season is another way to give feedback and it can be done in a way that's fun and makes everyone feel good about themselves.

- If you decide to do written evaluations, it's important to deliver it face-to-face with each player.

- The face-to-face player evaluation meetings can serve to motivate the player for the next season.

21 | Pre-Season Logistics

Things to do and decide:

☐ Set up a captain/co-captain schedule

☐ Will you have a parent volunteer to handle weekly emails/logistics?

☐ Team snacks for half time and/or after games?

☐ Is your daughter on the team? If yes, make sure you talk to her about your coaching role and how it will feel different during practices and games

First email to parents and players before the season begins:

☐ Information about practices (times/location) and game schedule.

☐ Pre-season parent meeting? If so, set a date/time/location.

☐ Ask for emails and cell phone numbers of all parents/guardians.

☐ Send out medical release forms for parents to give information on allergies and any medical conditions.

☐ If a player wears contact lenses, ask parents to bring an extra pair for the Team Emergency Medical Kit.

☐ Let them know there will be a weekly email reminder about upcoming practices and the game for that week if that is your frequency.

☐ Have the player contact the coach if she is going to miss practice or a game. Let them know that you are teaching your players self-advocacy by having them contact you (or the parent volunteer team manager) regarding any issues, concerns, or schedule conflicts.

Attach the following files for parents and players:

☐ Captain-Co-Captain Schedule

☐ Medical Release Form

☐ Parent Code of Conduct Contract

☐ Player Code of Conduct Contract

☐ Create Emergency Medical Kit

PRE-SEASON PLANNING –
NOTES

....

....

....

....

....

....

....

WE WANT TO HEAR FROM YOU!

We would love to hear about your experiences! Perhaps there is a coach that you want to recognize? Or you have a drill that you want to share that makes sport fun? Or maybe you have a question or concern? Let us know. Our website is **HowToCoachGirls.com**. We are on Twitter **@HowToCoachGirls**, Facebook **@HowToCoachGirls**, and Instagram **@HowToCoachGirls**.

Our website also has a **Coaches' Kit** of downloadable forms for Pre-Season Logistics.

Finally, if you are looking for a sport related non-profit to support for a team building event, we have a list.

COACHES'
BIOGRAPHIES

COACHES' BIOGRAPHIES

Fabian (Fabe) Ardila, President at MGA Sports Inc., and High Performance Court Coach, USA Volleyball

Fabian (Fabe) Ardila has coached volleyball for almost 30 years. In addition to having held the position of Assistant Coach for Harvard University, he has coached high school volleyball for both boys and girls at Newton South, Wellesley, Sacred Heart, and Weston High Schools. He currently coaches at the club level for Smash Volleyball, as well as at his own club, MGA. For the U.S.A. Women's National Volleyball Team, Fabe was a coach for the setters who competed at the Rio Olympics under Coach Karch Kiraly. He is currently working at U.S.A. Volleyball with high performance athletes, training future Olympians. Last, but certainly not least, he coached his three daughters who all play at an advanced level.

Brent Bode, Competitive Novice Girls Head Coach at Community Rowing Inc. (CRI), Boston, Massachusetts

Brent Bode has been coaching and teaching at Community Rowing, Inc. since 2010. He is Head Coach for the Competitive Youth Novice Girls program and Assistant Director of CRI's Coaching Education programming. Bode also coaches novice and intermediate adult rowers year-round and teaches fitness, strength, and conditioning to athletes of all ages. He holds a Master's degree in Exercise & Sports Studies from Smith College and is a long-time member of the National Strength and Conditioning Association.

Under Bode's direction, the Competitive Novice Girls team grew from 27 to more than 50 athletes in just three years.

Amanda Cromwell, Head Coach of Women's Soccer, UCLA

Amanda Cromwell is the Head Coach of UCLA's women's soccer, leading her team to the program's first-ever NCAA Championship after just eight months in the role. She was previously Head Coach for 14 years at the University of Central Florida, and Head Coach at the University of Maryland-Baltimore County.

At the University of Virginia, Cromwell was captain of the 1991 Cavaliers team that advanced to the Final Four. She was a two-time All-America selection, a finalist for the 1991 Hermann Trophy and a four-time All-Atlantic Coast Conference honoree. Cromwell is currently a member of the coaching staff sent by the State Department as an envoy to other countries to empower girls and women through soccer, and has served on the U.S. Soccer Board of Directors.

Katie Crowley, Head Coach of Women's Hockey, Boston College

Katie Crowley started as an Assistant Coach at Boston College in 2004, and was promoted to Head Coach in 2007. At the end of the 2014-15 season, Crowley was honored as National Coach of the Year.

Crowley won a gold medal in the 1998 Olympics in Nagano, Japan, a silver medal in the 2002 Games in Salt Lake City, and a bronze at the 2006 Games in Turin, Italy. She took home five consecutive silver medals in the World Championships (1997, 1999-2001, 2004), and a gold medal in 2005 with Team USA. In

2009, she and her 1998 Olympic teammates were enshrined in the U.S. Hockey Hall of Fame.

Crowley has worked with many national teams, and was named Head Coach of the 2010 Under-18 National Team.

Sarah Dacey, Head Coach of Women's Soccer, Barry University

Sarah Dacey joined Barry University as Head Coach in 2016 after spending the previous season as an Assistant Coach under Denise Brolly. Formerly, Dacey was the Head Coach at Babson College, as well as Club Head with FC Bolts and Pinecrest Premier Soccer Club. She served as an Assistant Coach at the University of Albany, Providence College, the University of Tennessee, and Boston College, where she helped lead the Eagles to the 2010 Women's College Cup.

Dacey played professionally for the WUSA's Carolina Courage and Boston Breakers until 2003. A four-year letterwinner and three-year starter under legendary coach Anson Dorrance at UNC, Dacey helped lead the Tar Heels' soccer program to three National Championships while earning Honorable Mention All-American honors in 1996.

Kelly Doton, Head Coach of Women's Field Hockey, Boston College

Kelly Doton became Head Coach of the Boston College field hockey program in 2015. She started as Associate Head Coach at Boston College in 2012, having previously coached at Indiana University. In Doton's four seasons, Boston College has posted double-digit wins each year and has advanced to the NCAA Tournament in the last three seasons from 2013 to 2015.

A 2004 graduate of Wake Forest, Doton was named the ACC Player of the Year in 2002, and was a two-time NFHCA First-Team All-American and a three-time All-ACC honoree during her career. Doton was a member of the U.S. Women's Senior National Team from 2005-10. In 2008, she was part of the U.S. squad that traveled to the Summer Olympics in Beijing, China.

Marc Gargaro , Boxing Trainer, Nonantum Boxing Club, Massachusetts

Marc Gargaro is a professional boxing trainer as well as USA Boxing Level 2 and AIBA Star 1 amateur boxing coach. He has extensive coaching experience at both the regional and national level, and has been selected as a national coach for both the men's and women's USA Boxing Elite National Team that competes in the Pan American and Olympic Games. Gargaro works with boxers of all ages, and has coached hundreds of fighters since co-founding Nonantum Boxing Club, around a quarter of whom have been women. He has personally trained and sent ten boxers to the National championships from his gym in Nonantum.

Erik Johnson, Head Coach of Women's Basketball, Boston College

Erik Johnson took over as Head Coach of women's basketball at Boston College in 2012, having previously coached at Denver from 2008 to 2012. In his first season, he took a team that was formerly 7-23 and finished 12-19 in the 2012-13 season.

Ainslee Lamb, Natick Middle School Coach and National Team Coach for USA Women's Field Hockey

Ainslee Lamb was Head Coach of the Yale University field hockey team from 1999 to 2003. In 2005, she became Head Coach of Boston College, where she remained for ten highly successful years. Under her lead, the Eagles achieved a winning record. She currently coaches Natick Middle School girls field hockey as well as various national teams for the USA Field Hockey program.

Prior to college, Lamb was a member of both the 1990 World Cup team and Canadian National team from 1987-92, where she competed in the Junior World Cup, the Olympic qualifying tournament and two Four Nation Tournaments. A 1994 graduate of the University of Toronto, Lamb was a three-year field hockey letter winner, and helped lead the team to a national championship in 1988.

Dave Lombardo, Head Coach of Women's Soccer, James Madison University

Dave Lombardo is the first and only Head Coach in James Madison women's soccer history, completing his 27th season at the helm in 2016 with 22 winning seasons. Prior to James Madison University, Lombardo was Head Coach at Keene State College from 1981 to 1987. He was the early architect of an Owl women's soccer team that would go on to prominence at both the regional and national levels. He is the sixth Keene State College coach to be inducted into the Alumni-Athletic Hall of Fame. He has the seventh most wins amongst active Division I coaches.

Mary-Frances Monroe, Head Coach of Women's Soccer, University of Miami

Mary-Frances Monroe took over as Head Soccer Coach at University of Miami in 2016, having previously been the Head Coach of the University of Albany. A highly respected player and instructor, Monroe competed on the field with the Boston Breakers in the WPSL Elite League as recently as the 2012 season.

Monroe and her coaching staff won the 2009 America East Co-Coaching Staff of the Year honors in just her fourth year at the helm. During that season, the Great Danes earned the first Division I postseason berth in program history. In 2010, the Great Danes finished with a 10-8-2 record under Monroe's direction, the first winning season for the program since 1988.

Monroe achieved success on the international level as a player, earning several caps with the United States Women's National Team.

Ashley Obrest, Head Coach of Women's Softball, Boston College

Ashley Obrest returned to Boston College in 2011 as Head Softball Coach where she is still in the school's record book for career runs batted in, as well as single-season on-base percentage and walk. Under her coaching, in 2014 the Eagles won a program-best 12 ACC games.

Obrest was at Colgate University prior to rejoining Boston College, first as Assistant Coach, before being promoted to Head Coach in July 2010. She set a school record for most wins by a first year Head Coach (27) and led the Raiders to a regular season Patriot League title. Previously, Obrest served as an Assistant Coach at Concordia University in Chicago and a private hitting and catching instructor for the Chicago White Sox Training Academy.

Randy Thomas, Head Coach Women's Track and Field, Boston College

Randy Thomas is the Program Director of the women's cross

country and track and field teams at Boston College. A former world record holder, he has guided the women's cross country squad to 16 NCAA Championships in the past 24 seasons. Overall, Thomas, who served exclusively as the school's cross country coach during the first seven years of his tenure, has produced a total of 52 All-America selections, four national junior champions and one Pan-American Games gold medalist. His coaching honors include New England Intercollegiate Amateur Athletic Association as the Division I Women's Coach of the Year, and the 2001 Track and Field Association National Cross Country Coach of the Year.

Acacia Walker, Head Coach of Women's Lacrosse, Boston College

Acacia Walker has been coaching women's lacrosse at Boston College since 2011, first as Associate Head Coach, before being promoted to Head Coach in 2012. In 2014, she brought the Boston College women's lacrosse team to their first ever Final Four. Prior to coaching the Eagles, Walker was the Associate Head Coach at the University of Massachusetts. She was also an Assistant Coach at Northwestern, where the Wildcats won three consecutive NCAA National Championships and three consecutive American Lacrosse Conference titles.

Walker was the youngest member of the World Championship U19 Team that won gold in Perth, Australia in 1999. She also won a gold medal with the U.S. Women's Senior National Lacrosse Team at the 2009 World Cup in Prague, and was a member of the 2010-11 U.S. National Team. She was named the Division I Intercollegiate Women's Lacrosse Coaches Association National Coach of the Year in 2017.

Chandra Wisneski, Nordic Ski Instructor, Newton North High School, Massachusetts

Chandra Wisneski began Nordic Skiing as a freshman in high school. She joined the Nordic team at the University of Maine at Presque Isle and studied a dual major in Cross Country Ski Coaching and Athletic Training. After graduating, she was part of the coaching team for the New Zealand National Development Team. She furthered her education with a chiropractic degree, and continued coaching Nordic Ski as the Ski School Director at Weston Ski Track. She is the Newton North High School Nordic Ski coach for both the girls' and boys' teams. In just two years, the team grew from 38 to 58 members.

INDEX

INDEX

T

U

V

W

CPSIA information can be obtained
at www.ICGtesting.com
Printed in the USA
LVHW01s2336230418
574641LV00021B/699/P